Juan: We will never find a way to thank you enough for what you have done ... especially for the poor, for the unemployed, for the migrants, for the young. Thank you! Keep hitting hard!
Vicente Fox, President of Mexico. A personal letter.

Juan Hernández is a champion in fighting for the underserved, the marginalized, the poor. His passion for migrants was evident as he served in the presidential cabinet. Only if we work together, as Juan's book insists, will we create a better relationship between the peoples of Mexico and the U.S. during these times of great debate, great fear and great confusion.
Marta Sahagún de Fox, The First Lady of Mexico

I have had the joy of working with Juan in Mexico's "peaceful revolution" in the year 2000. I have witnessed his love for democracy, his love for people and untiring compassionate spirit. This book will not only touch minds, it will change hearts. The U.S. and Mexico must learn to understand and appreciate each other as friends, as partners, as family. This is what Juan's book is all about.
Juan Carlos Romero Hicks,
Governor of the State of Guanajuato, Mexico

Juan Hernández is a poet, scholar, university professor, analyst, bi-cultural interpreter and a restless political activist. He is undoubt-edly the best equipped North American to carry the torch that will shed light as to how North America can grow as a community that will generate welfare for those living in Mexico, the United States and Canada. This book is about Juan's vision, portrayed in docu-mented experiences of migrant heroes who work every day to build a global society with a North American perspective.
José Luis Romero Hicks, Law Offices of Romero & Galindo,
former Cabinet Member under President Vicente Fox

I know no one better qualified to speak on the issues of Mexican immigrants than Juan Hernandez. His love of America, his exten-sive experience in the United States and his close involvement with the president of Mexico, Vicente Fox, inform his rich and passionate understanding of the hurts, rights, and needs of the Mexican worker. Juan Hernandez brings a passionate, principled, and realistic voice to the complex issues confronting Mexican and U.S. relations on the subject of immigration. Hernandez is an important voice on behalf of the great variety of Mexican immigrants among us.

Dr. Robert Sloan, Chancellor of Baylor University

Dr. Hernandez writes about a New North America where a new spirit of cooperation and democracy will flourish. He is, indeed, the personification of the New North American moving freely across borders and cultures to build a bridge to a better future for all.

James Keyes, President and CEO, 7-Eleven, Inc.

Juan Hernandez has always been a bridge between Mexico and the United States. Born in the United States, Hernandez made history when he was appointed by Vicente Fox as Director of the Office of the President for Mexicans Abroad. With enormous energy he promoted the rights of Mexican immigrants living in the United States and made sure that they were properly represented and taken care of in Mexico City. He was a privileged participant to the arrival of a true democracy in Mexico in the year 2000. His book is testimony of this unprecedented effort and reflects with a direct, honest language the complexity of the relationship between 'distant neighbors.' This is a book of a very pragmatic poet who knows both countries intimately and tells it like it is. His insights into binational relations are unparalleled. Hernandez has been a witness to what most Mexicans and Americans have never seen.

Jorge Ramos, Author and Senior Anchorman, Univisión News

"The New American Pioneers" is a fascinating, straightforward and provocative read that makes an important contribution toward breaking down historic walls of misconception and building greater mutual understanding and respect between us.

Dr. Thomas S. Fortson, President/CEO, Promise Keepers

The Hispanic growth in our country is no doubt a paramount issue. The bishops of the United States have accurately called immigrants: "a blessing for our country and a divine gift for the Catholic Church." This book is also a blessing for our country because it will enlighten many minds and change many hearts. Thank you, Juan.

Fr. Stephan Jasso, All Saints Catholic Church,
Fort Worth, Texas

Juan Hernández is a convincing, passionate, and compassionate voice in favor of serving the New Americans. He has convinced me that the Church should become involved in this effort, and I am sure you will be convinced as well.

Rev. Robert Morris, Senior Pastor of Gateway Church,
Southlake, Texas

Californians know Juan Hernandez. He speaks a message few are willing to deliver. He invites us to a debate few are willing to approach. Read this book. The issues are complex: immigration, US-Mexico relations, advancing Hispanics in America. Hernandez is passionate and his vision contagious!

Rev. Bayless Conley, Senior Pastor of Cottonwood
Christian Center, Los Alamitos, California

I know of no other with the credentials and experience to tackle the controversial issues related to immigration than Dr. Juan Hernandez. I call him, "the hero of the Mexican immigrant." He is giving us exactly what we need — a proactive analysis of a very difficult issue.

Rev. Daniel de León, Senior Pastor of Templo Calvario,
Santa Ana, California

A fresh work based on convictions and personal experience. Dr. Juan Hernández presents an open mind and an open heart. This book provides a realistic perspective on building the New America with New Americans, without losing our nation's principles.

Rev. Luis López, President of Florida Alliance of Hispanic Evangelical Churches and Hispanic Christian Church Association of Central Florida

Juan Hernandez has written a brilliant new book which redefines for all of us what it means to be Americans. Like the new American pioneers Dr. Hernandez chronicles, this important work by the hemisphere's foremost voice on immigration goes bravely across new frontiers of this critical issue shaping our world for the 21st Century.

Rob Allyn, International Political Consultant

Juan Hernandez is right! There is nothing less rational than the entrenched American opposition to immigration.

Dick Morris, Author and Fox News Channel Political Analyst

Sometimes in life, we meet someone whom we both like and respect immediately. Dr. Juan Hernandez and I became acquainted shortly after Vicente Fox was elected President of Mexico. He was asked by the President-elect to tackle initiatives that would make life better for Mexicans on both sides of the border. Juan and I met many times and dreamt that someday all those not using the formal financial services sector in America would do so for all of the right reasons: safety, reasonable fees, inexpensive credit, and wealth accumulation.

Back in the early 1900's, the mills and factories in the eastern section of this country imported Europeans to work the many unskilled labor jobs that they could not fill with the existing citizenry. When here and working, they experienced much of the difficulty that new Americans face today. Crooks followed them on payday and stole their money after the paychecks were cashed.

In the 1920's a crusade was launched by Roy Bergengren who marched around the country promoting laws so that credit unions could reach out to these underserved workers and their families.

Like Bergengren, Juan Hernández has started a crusade. He literally marches across America talking to credit union groups, chambers of commerce, legislators and community organizations while spreading the word about the needs of new Americans and the way credit unions are positioned to help. He has found his calling, and we are better for it!!

Richard Ensweiler, Chairman of the Credit Union National Association and CEO and President of the Texas Credit Union League

For over five years, Juan Hernández and I have had an ongoing conversation on the very complex and controversial issues related to U.S.-Mexico migration. We have not always agreed. Nevertheless, we share a belief that immigration reform is possible and that four key areas must be addressed if this goal is to be attained: The undocumented (or unauthorized) population; immigration enforcement; labor market issues; and immigrant integration.

Regarding the unauthorized population, it must be stated that this large and growing population represents a fundamental breakdown in the rule of law. The overwhelming majority of the adult unauthorized population is working and most live in households with some members who have legal status. They have a profound economic impact on U.S. labor markets, communities and their home countries to which they send billions of dollars each year.

It is understandable that many in the U.S. are concerned about immigration enforcement and security. Nevertheless, tough border enforcement has not been equal to the task of stopping the flow of illegal immigration. Furthermore, our current policy invites people to take great personal risk to defeat border controls for the payoff of ready access to the U.S. labor market.

Regarding labor markets: using immigration effectively will be a key ingredient for America's long-term economic prosperity and competitiveness. The U.S. needs fundamental changes in existing immigration criteria.

Finally, I must mention immigrant integration. The nation's immigrant integration policies are ad hoc, fragmentary, underfunded and fall largely to state and local governments. The most pressing issues relate to the large numbers coming in, geographical concentration and dispersion, skill and education levels, child poverty, the capacity of institutions that have historically played a role in integration, and the status of the social safety net.

As congressmen, migration experts and the U.S. and Mexican peoples search for answers to the complex migration issues, "The New American Pioneers" is a voice that must be included.

Demetrios G. Papademetriou, President, The Migration Policy Institute, Washington, DC

The
New American
Pioneers

Why are we afraid of Mexican immigrants?

Juan Hernández

PUBLISHING

The New American Pioneers

Why are we afraid of Mexican immigrants?

Contact:

Juan Hernandez
PMB 312
4750 Bryant Irvin Rd. Ste. 808
Fort Worth, TX 76132-3611

24 Hour TV Network: www.juanhernandez.tv
Website: www.juanhernandez.org

ISBN 1-56229-052-5

Pneuma Life Publishing
P. O. Box 10612
Lanham, MD 20721
1-800-727-3218
www.pneumalife.com

"America is a stronger and better nation because of the hard work and the faith and the entrepreneurial spirit of immigrants... One of the primary reasons America became a great power in the twentieth century is because we welcomed the talent and the character and the patriotism of immigrant families...

As a Texan, I have known many immigrant families, mainly from Mexico, and I've seen what they add to our country. They bring to America the values of faith in God, love of family, hard work, and self-reliance; the values that made us a great nation...."

—*President George W. Bush*
January 7, 2004 speech

Dedication

This book is dedicated to the migrants in my family:

My father Francisco Hernández who immigrated to the U.S.

My mother Mary Clay Senter who immigrated to Mexico.

My brothers and sisters - Margie, Nina, Francisco, Daniel and Mary - who share my pocho confusions.

My wife, Estela, and my children, Estela, John, Laura and Mariana, who have followed me in my constant migration through literary adventures, political campaigns, dreams and spiritual journey.

Acknowledgements

This book is greatly influenced by friends and colleagues such as Jorge Bustamante, Alejandro Carrillo-Castro, Jorge Castañeda, Xochitl Castañeda, Wayne Cornelius, Alberto Dávila, Howard Duncan, Agustín Escobar, Jorge Durand, Rafael Fernández de Castro, Luin Goldring, Rodolfo Hernández, Raúl Hinojosa, Khalid Koser, Amanda Levinson, Douglas Massey, Jesús Martínez, Oscar Martínez, Rubén Martínez, Porfirio Muñoz Ledo, José Pagán, Demetrios Papademetriou, Jose Angel Pescador, Neil Ruiz, Jorge Santibañez, Yossi Shain, Joanne Van Selm, Robert Smith, Omar de la Torre, Rodolfo Tuirán, Julie Weise, among many others. Some of the experts mentioned above developed the concepts which are highlighted in the oral histories. Their research, and in many cases their friendship, have been the point of departure for the humanistic work before you.

Some of the friends who have believed in me, against general wisdom, are Gabriel Acero, Victor Almeida, David R. Ayon, Bayless Conley, Dick Ensweiler, Ben Ferrell, Roberto González Moreno, Jim Kerby, Danny de León, Luis López, José Natera, Jay McCarley, Horacio McCoy, Jorge Mettey, Jorge Delgado, Dick Morris, Robert Morris, Francisco Ochoa, José Ortega, Ramiro Peña, José Luis Romero Hicks, Juan Carlos Romero Hicks, Luis Alberto Villaseñor, Agustín Villaseñor, Hobson Wildenthal, Gary Williams, Marcos Witt, and… Vicente Fox.

Contents

Foreward

Juan Hernandez is right! There is nothing less rational than the entrenched American opposition to immigration, particularly from Mexico. Immigration, the historic mainstay of American growth and prosperity, remains to this day the fundamental ingredient in our economic and social viability. Its restriction or curtailment would do great injury to us all and would represent a cruel closing of the doors of opportunity in the face of many hardworking and deserving people.

First some facts. The United States population is relatively stable. It grows by a little more than one percent each year — about 3.3 million people. About half comes from American births minus deaths and the other half from immigration — legal and illegal.

The U.S. is not overcrowded nor will a growth rate of about 1% annually trigger overcrowding.

The biggest problem that the other nations of the developed world — in Japan and Western Europe — face is depopulation, not over-crowding. Current estimates suggest that by 2050 Spain will shrink from its current level of 41 million people to 32 million. Russia is looking at a decrease from 145 million to only slightly more than 100 million. Japan's current population of 125 million is likewise expected to drop to 100 million by the middle of the century.

In these shrinking nations, growth is hobbled endangering pension systems, undermining the capacity for national growth and power, and even raises the looming threat of national extinction.

Immigration is vital for America's future for many good reasons:

Immigration keeps us young. The average age of immigrants is well below the national average. This infusion of new, young blood into our national arteries makes America the exception in a world of shrinking, stagnating developed nations. The energy and commitment to hard work of our new immigrants contributes mightily to our national sense of vitality.

Immigration helps protect our pension systems. With the ratio of employed people to retirees expected to shrink to 3:1 in twenty years, the growth of a population of young working people will be a big part of being able to keep the promise of Social Security to the elderly of the future. Even today, immigrants — legal and illegal — contribute billions to Social Security which they are unlikely ever to draw upon, subsidizing the rest of us.

Immigration keeps down inflation. With a national unemployment rate under five percent, the possibility of a national labor shortage severely impedes our capacity for economic growth. With an upward pressure from wages, the Federal Reserve Board would be unable to maintain the current environment of low interest rates which fuels high economic growth. Most economists suggest that a four percent unemployment rate is the equivalent of a zero rate. They hold that four percent is the normal rate for the usual turnover in any labor market. When an economy runs out of workers, the risk of wage driven inflation is enough to cool down any efforts at economic stimulus.

Immigration improves our quality of life. The work that immigrants do needs doing. Otherwise they wouldn't be hired to do it. Whether it is gardening, manufacturing, or other low skill jobs, the immigrant community labors in the hot sun to improve our standard of living and deserves our respect and gratitude.

Immigration is the best anti-poverty program. With four percent of the world's population and twenty-nine percent of the world's wealth, the United States has an affirmative obligation to help the poor of other countries. But Americans are rightly suspicious of government foreign aid which usually ends up in the pockets of petty dictators in foreign banana republics. However, the remittances sent home by immigrants who toil in the United States go directly into the homes of the poor without government bureaucracy or meddling. The almost $20 billion sent home by Mexicans working in the United States represents the greatest source of national wealth than any sector of the Mexican economy except for oil revenues. It amounts to a grant of about $200 for every man, woman and child in Mexico each year — often a very high percentage of the disposable income of these impoverished people.

With all of these advantages, why does an obdurate nativism stand in the way of immigration? Most of the criticism distinguishes between legal and illegal immigration. But immigration laws are hopelessly antiquated and are designed for a nation beset by chronic unemployment — a condition that no longer exists and hasn't for more than a decade.

But what if a recession comes again? Won't immigrants then be thrown into competition for scarce jobs? The fact is that the unemployment rate has dropped during each of the past three recessions due to the underlying strength of the American economy. The recession of the early 80's peaked at a jobless rate of 10 percent. The recession of the early 90's led to unemployment as high as 8 percent. But the economic crisis which gripped us in the early years of this decade led to unemployment which peaked at 6 percent.

Even in a recession, immigrants are not going to represent competition for the jobs most Americans want.

And what of the legal aspects of immigration? The answer is simple: Change the laws. It is artificial for the United States to restrict its legal immigration to the range of only about one million people per year. It is in the interest of the immigrants — and, more importantly, all Americans — that we let more people enter our nation legally.

Some oppose immigration because they fear that the newly arrived Hispanics will remain clustered in an inert voting and cultural block that will not assimilate as so many other tens of millions of immigrants have done. But the evidence suggests that Hispanics are entering the melting pot as surely as have other groups. Significantly, for example, while African-Americans continue to block vote for the Democratic Party (90-10 in 2000 and 89-11 in 2004), Hispanics are showing their assimilation by voting 55-45 for Kerry in 2004 after supporting Gore by 65-35 in the previous contest. While the political numbers do not matter to our consideration in this volume, the assimilation they evidence does.

Linguistically, recent surveys indicate that only about one-third of all Hispanic households in the United States have only limited knowledge of English. Another third are fluent in our national language but say they tend to speak Spanish at home. And another third speak English at home and outside. This is the pattern of all immigrant groups for the last two hundred years.

We need to stop thinking with our prejudices and begin looking at our real self-interest. And let's remember that all but a handful of we Americans came from families that came from somewhere else!

Dick Morris
International Political Consultant,
Fox News Channel Political Analyst

Introduction

The Heroes Among Us

Breathes there the man with soul so dead,
Who never to himself hath said,
This is my own, my native land!

As a poet, I appreciate the beauty and passion of these lines by the nineteenth century Scotsman, Sir Walter Scott. "Born in the USA," I am grateful for the privilege to call the United States my home, to feel a swell of pride when I hear the stirring climax to the U.S. national anthem paying tribute to "the land of the free and the home of the brave." On the other hand, I am very proud to have participated in a presidential campaign that brought democracy to Mexico. I am grateful that Mexico "adopted" me, and allowed me to serve in the historic Fox administration. Finally, I am grateful that both nations have constitutions allowing me to serve, without conflict of interest, in the land of my father and the land of my mother.

In recent years I have felt keen admiration for the heroes among us—for the firemen, police officers, and willing volunteers who sought to save lives from the blazing infernos of New York City's World Trade Center twin towers (and Washington D.C.'s Pentagon) after the infamous attacks on September 11, 2001. I have also watched with admiration the heroes (including many undocumented workers) who are bringing life back to cities devastated by recent hurricanes. All through the long months of search-and-rescue, clean-up and reconstruction the heroics continue.

The significance and impact of these tragic events cannot be overstated. The terrorist and nature attacks on our own soil changed the U.S.— and the world—irrevocably and forever. Nothing can ever be the same again.

But I am also proud to be "from" Mexico, the land where my father was born, grew up, and worked. I am proud to have participated with the heroes who brought democracy to Mexico in 2000. I am humbled by the opportunity that was given me to serve on President Vicente Fox's cabinet. I appreciate the long history and rich culture of Mexico—in President George Bush's words, "the values of faith in God, love of family, hard work, and self-reliance." I am proud to have two cultures—to be called a Latino, a Hispanic, a Mexican American.

And having witnessed firsthand the difficulties and challenges that have forced Mexican workers to leave friends and home to seek employment in the U.S. to help provide for their families, I understand full well why President Vicente Fox calls them "heroes—our brightest and best!" The overwhelming majority of these immigrants are good people, beautiful people, honest and hardworking, full of life and laughter, faith and love. I have worked with them and admired them on both sides of the border, before and after they became immigrants to the U.S.

Foreign Here and There

The first time I was called "foreigner," someone said it in Spanish. The first time I was an immigrant, I was an American living in Mexico.

When I was a young child, my family moved from Fort Worth, Texas—which for me was a country and a universe of its own—to Guanajuato, Mexico. Though I was born in Texas, Guanajuato was where my father, Francisco Heránndez, serenaded an American exchange student, my mother Mary Clay Senter, until she fell in love with him.

And so, I became the American kid in school, my blond hair setting me apart from the other students in Guanajuato. Then, a few years later when my family moved to Texas, I became the Mexican kid in school back in Fort Worth. I had forgotten much of my English vocabulary, and my Mexican accent was pronounced. My third-grade teacher, Ms. White, sent me to the corner with comic books and novels by Louis L'Amour and Agatha Christie until I learned how to read English.

One Mexican immigrant I know says asking him to choose between the United States and Mexico would be like asking him to choose between his mother and father. For me, the metaphor is not metaphorical.

Mexico and the United States met each day in my home—just as they do today from Staten Island, New York to Earlimart, California; from Omaha, Nebraska to San Antonio, Texas; from big cities to small, rural towns like Mexico, Missouri. Sometimes my parents would misunderstand one another and I would be the interpreter, the bicultural go-between.

"No, Dad," I sometimes say to this day. "You're thinking of this in terms of Mexico. But that's not how things are done in the United States." Occasionally I have to do the same for my mother, explaining my Mexican father's culture to her.

I have never had to choose between my parents, and I have never had a reason to choose between Mexico and the United States. And in that simple observation, I believe, lies the contribution of this book. Most stories about immigrants to the United States feature the "choice" as a turning point in the narrative. Cutting ties with the country of origin in order to become an American is the climax of the story.

I do not doubt that this traditional story reflects the experiences of millions of immigrants, but in this book I hope to propose a new way of telling immigrant stories, and in particular Mexican immigrant stories. I want to remain honest to both a personal and political reality—Mexico is just over the border on the same North American continent, and migrants do retain their ties. They stay connected to their families, and they send billions of dollars each year home to Mexico.

Yes, many of them do prefer Spanish to English and will all of their lives. When they do become U.S. citizens and participate in politics, their motivation for doing so tends to come from their experiences as immigrants, and their impulse to correct the injustices they see committed against Latinos and other immigrants. In all these ways, I believe they are not misfits, but model American immigrants.

I am not the first to propose that bicultural and transnational practices have been a crucial part of immigrants' lives throughout U.S. history. Multicultural historians have re-told the American story with a focus on the contributions that immigrants have made to the building of the nation, and with great sensitivity to these immigrants' continuing connections to the countries and families they left behind.

Dealing with the Downside

But let's be completely frank and honest. The influx of immigrant workers—many of them with no legal entry documents—is not without problems. With millions of migrant workers already here, and hundreds of thousands more coming each year, some U.S. citizens are frustrated by their sheer increase in numbers. In addition since 9/11, there are some legitimate concerns about border security. A "coyote" human smuggling industry has sprung up, many times with tragic consequences. On average, one or two immigrants die every day in the desert, rivers, or mountains, trying to get to that job that is waiting in the U.S. With tighter control of border crossing checkpoints, many undocumented immigrants who formerly would come and go are afraid to risk leaving the U.S., so they stay longer. In some states, government officials claim educational budgets and medical care facilities have been overloaded. Some U.S. citizens have lost jobs to immigrants. Some labor leaders are concerned that pay levels for others are kept too low by the abundance of Mexican workers.

I am aware of these and other related problems that are complex and serious. There are no simple solutions. Our present immigration system is not just outdated—it is broken and we must fix it. We must stop closing our eyes to reality and seriously seek strong solutions. The solutions must be fair to U.S. employers, to U.S. workers, and to immigrants. *More patches won't do.* And shooting at shadows is not the answer.

I believe this nation can and will find answers to these problems. I believe U.S. leaders can create immigration laws that, in President Bush's words, will make us "a more compassionate, more humane, and stronger country."[1] Already responsible men from both political parties—on the left and the right—are making good faith proposals and first steps to bring order out of the chaos of the current immigration policy.

Democratic leaders like Ted Kennedy, Joe Leiberman, Dick Gephardt, and Howard Dean have suggested providing U.S. citizenship to responsible immigrants with no criminal records. Republicans like John Cornyn, John McCain, and George W. Bush have proposed temporary worker programs that would create a more orderly flow of immigrant workers to match available jobs and require a return home after work visas ended. President Bush's Hispanic nephew, George Prescott Bush is also pushing for legalization of current immigrant workers and a stronger temporary work visa program. Bush is the son of Florida governor Jeb Bush and mother, Columba, originally from Mexico. In fact, his grandfather, José María Garnica, was a migrant worker from the state of Guanajuato.

In May 2005, McCain and Kennedy introduced a new bill proposing broad immigration overhaul with a multistep path to citizenship for undocumented immigrants and a new program for future foreign workers.[2] The measure has bipartisan support, but it has also stirred vigorous opposition.

There will be political battles and tough sledding as these and other measures are debated. Progress may be slower than we would like, but I have faith that suitable solutions can and will be found.

A Clearer View of Reality

In my work with Mexico's Vicente Fox—during his historic election campaign and as a U.S. American-born member of his cabinet as Special Advisor for Mexicans Abroad—I learned an important lesson early on. This lesson is that it's not about me. The presidential campaign was not about me, the office I held was not about me, and the book I write today is not about my importance.

When I met with Mexican citizens during the election and later as the president's representative, sometimes a person would see the U.S. American part of me and say, "What are you, a Gringo, doing here?" The correct answer to that question was always, "You are right, this is not about me. *You are the important one!* Will you please allow me the honor of being of service to you?"

In this book, I will strive to maintain this same posture. Please do not view me as an expert or authority trying to tell you how it is. This is not about what I know or have experienced—it is about you and I attempting to come to a better understanding of a watershed issue of monumental importance in the history of the United States and of North America. Together we can help influence the thinking of twenty-first century U.S. Americans and, with your contemporaries, shape the course of North America and the world in the months and years ahead.

So I will try to identify some of the important issues and underscore what is at stake. I will share what I have learned and, as much as possible, separate the facts from the biases, prejudices, and special interests. As a university educator with the unique distinction of having been reared by a Mexican father and a U.S. American mother while living in both countries, I will present the issues before us as objectively as I know how. I will tell you my story and share my concerns, hopes, and dreams. My purpose or goal is for you and I to see and understand the big picture a little better as we work ourselves through this complex maze.

There is no better way to visualize the realities of immigrants' lives than to read their own words. Yet, oral histories have only just begun to assume the task of directly challenging the dominant—and woefully incomplete—view of U.S. immigration history. This book seeks to do it differently—to find a way of telling stories that create a new American immigrant narrative, while also acknowledging that the daily lives of these brave souls challenge even this new version. The diversity of the Mexican immigrant experience—and the even greater diversity in the way he or she assimilates and responds to a new environment—is reflected in these testimonies.

My own story—like "Mr. Smith Goes to Washington," or should I say, "Señor Hernández Goes to Mexico City"—provides the perspective for a unique overview and a personal rapport with the remarkable people who have sacrificed everything to go north so their families can have a better life. They are VIPs, very important paisanos, both for the citizens of Mexico and the citizens of the United States—for all the people of North America!

Dr. Juan Hernández
Fort Worth, Texas

1 President George W. Bush, speech proposing new temporary worker program and immigration policy reform, January 7, 2004.

2 2005 Secure America and Orderly Immigration Act, introduced May 12, 2005 in U.S. Senate by John McCain and Ted Kennedy, and in the House of Representatives by Representatives Jeff Flake, R-AZ; Jim Kolbe, R-AZ; and Luis V. Gutierrez, D-IL.

Chapter 1

A Gringo in Mexico's Los Pinos

From my youth, living in both the U.S. and Mexico, I became keenly aware that my two beloved countries, although geographical neighbors, were worlds apart in many ways. At times I was not completely comfortable in either place, not sure I was totally accepted either. Even as I served as a go-between to overcome the occasional cultural misunderstandings of my own parents, early on I had a desire to become a bridge between the distinct, yet equally-valuable cultures that nurtured me.

My father was a Mexican attorney. He dropped out of law school when he got married, and after creating a family of six—they ended up with a family of eight—he went back to finish law school. His law practice was in Mexico, and he often took me as a child to visit jails and penitentiaries where he helped defendants no one else would defend. I would bring my guitar, sing songs, and play basketball with the inmates. My father told me, "These are people who may or may not have committed mistakes in their lives. They deserve a chance to tell their side of the story." Today he lives in Fort Worth where he translates in federal courts and works with U.S. American attorneys on matters of immigration law.

My mother is an interesting personality. She went from Fort Worth to Mexico to study Spanish and art when it was very uncommon to travel south of the border. When she fell in love with a Mexican, everyone was against the couple's getting married, both the family in Mexico as well as the family in Texas.

Mother is an artist and the family's spiritual leader. She first became a follower of the God of Love, she says, and then "discovered

Jesus." A very Anglo looking woman, she would ride on city buses and purposely sit next to African Americans just to create a stir among the whites and demonstrate her view of love and Christianity. Although we were certainly not wealthy, while living in Fort Worth, mother hired a lady to babysit us kids and clean the house while she worked for Justin Boots. One day mother's car wouldn't start, so when our African American baby-sitter arrived, mother asked her boyfriend who dropped her off to give her a ride to town. He was driving a truck, and she took great delight in having him slow down at every intersection so she could wave to neighbors, making sure they saw her riding with a black man. That was in the 1950's. Today my mother is an artist, who paints mostly scenes from Mexico. One of her more controversial works, related to the deaths of immigrants in the Arizona desert, hangs in Los Pinos (Mexico's White House).

Mother made sure I learned to respect African Americans and recognized the importance of their struggle for basic civil rights. Even at my young age, I could see how influential Dr. King and other black leaders were, and I admired the changes they were championing in our country. I never expected that I personally would have the opportunity to meet many important world leaders.

While teaching at the University of Texas in Dallas in 1996, I invited the newly elected governor of my childhood state of Guanajuato to speak at a Center for U.S.-Mexico Studies I had just launched. I had never met Vicente Fox, but my lifetime friends, Luis Alberto Villaseñor, Juan Carlos Romero Hicks, and José Luis Romero Hicks said he was "different from any other politician in Mexico." To my surprise, he accepted my invitation. So I coordinated three days of meetings for him in Texas, including his first meeting with George W. Bush, then governor of Texas.

An Historic Introduction

I had met George W. Bush previously at a couple of meetings related to education in Texas. He has an incredible memory—the second time we met he said, "You are that blond Hernandez." As we walked into the governor's office in Austin, I experienced my first encounter with the pushing and shoving that goes on when everybody wants to be close to power. I had to stick my hand out several times before I was acknowledged as part of the group. No one seemed to remember that I was the one who had coordinated the meeting.

After a couple of photographs, the two governors went into closed chambers. Fox's aides, U.S. Ambassador to Mexico James Jones, and I waited outside. We remained very quiet because parts of the conversation between the two governors could be heard, although we couldn't really understand all that was being said. The scheduled meeting of fifteen minutes went on for about an hour. Governor Bush's secretaries and staff were ready to leave since it was after five o'clock. But behind the big doors we could hear that the two men had really hit it off. They were both laughing and, at one point, it sounded as if they were throwing things at each other.

When the two governors came out, we said our goodbyes and boarded limousines. I asked Fox, "What did you two talk about?"

He said they had discussed the need for fairer migration laws and the development of migrant sending areas in Mexico. Fox said he had offered to raise $20 million from businessmen in Guanajuato if Bush would raise the same amount to start a pilot program which would be of mutual benefit to the state of Texas and the state of Guanajuato.

"What was Bush's response?" I asked. "How did he answer?" (I learned later that one shouldn't ask so many questions about closed-door meetings, but I was new at this.)

Fox just smiled and said, "He said he wished it were so easy to raise money in the U.S. but said we should discuss it further. I did not expect him to be so casual. I think we can work with him!"

So I concluded that the two hit it off very well, beginning a very cordial and lasting friendship that became even more significant a few years later when both men were candidates for the presidency of their respective countries. (During the campaigns I would keep both governors informed on how well the other was doing. I am not sure how, but the Karl Roves and the Condoleezza Rices all had my cell phone number and called often.)

My childhood friends were right. Vicente Fox was very different. He was very tall, very "American" looking, and very informal (always wearing boots, a western belt buckle, and never a tie). He has a booming baritone voice. And when you shake hands, his huge hands wrap around yours as he pulls you into his vision for bringing change in Mexico.

At one point during the trip, after he had given a speech to students on the Austin campus of the University of Texas, we got into the limousine and he immediately asked, "What did you think of my speech?"

"You are really good at answering the questions of the students," I answered.

"I asked you what you thought of my speech!" he boomed.

"I just want to emphasize that you were so natural in the question-and-answer sessions and with the media..."

"So you didn't like my speech!" he interrupted, refusing to let me go.

"Well, to be honest," I replied, "it sounded like a freshman paper. Who wrote it for you?"

Fox was sitting in the front passenger seat. I was sitting behind the driver. He looked back at me with a look I learned not to mess with during the next few years. He threw the script for the speech to me and said, "Well, why don't you fix it?"

From that moment we had an agreement—I would always tell him the truth as I saw it, and he would always challenge me to fix what I told him was not right. (I stayed up all night re-writing that speech, which he purposely would never read!)

The trip was a huge success despite the fact that I had never organized anything like it before. We had a great variety of meetings with business leaders, politicians, community leaders, and migrant groups. The event got Univision TV coverage, scores of interviews and a front cover picture in the Dallas Morning News. Fox was a big hit; people just flocked to him. Word of mouth made attendance at the meetings grow more and more as the days went on.

As Fox was going up the steps to board his little government jet at Love Field, about to return to Mexico, he asked me, "Have you got any other ideas?"

I had written down four ideas in my DayTimer just in case he asked. "Yes," I said. "You are an incredible salesperson for your state! You should be coming up here several times a year; you should open trade offices in U.S. cities; you should have a warehouse…"

"Okay," he said, and waited for my response.

"What do you mean, 'okay?'" I questioned.

"Do it!"

"Look, Vicente, I am a poet. I have nothing to do with trade…."

"No te rajes! Let's meet in Guanajuato next week and organize something. Okay?"

The thought of going to the governor's palace, being with Fox again, re-visiting Guanajuato and seeing my childhood friends—it all sounded great. So I said, "Okay."

The next week in Guanajuato he challenged me to work as his representative opening Guanajuato Trade Offices in several U.S. cities to promote commerce and economic development for his state.

I again tried to graciously decline, explaining again that I was a poet not a businessman, and that the success of his visit to Texas was really due to my friend, Juan Carlos Romero Hicks and Ambassador Jones, but he would not take no for an answer. So I took on the challenge, making presentations to government leaders in numerous cities, and accompanying Fox during his visits to the U.S.

With the help and encouragement of many people, Fox opened an office in Dallas and then offices in New York, Chicago, and Los Angeles. We set up a warehouse of Mexican crafts and western goods in Dallas. We had long hours of conversations together. I started giving him books to read by political experts like Dick Morris. Vicente started asking me to check out international political advisers such as Rob Allyn. His children began coming to stay for vacations in our home.

A Vision for a new Mexico

As our friendship grew, it became apparent that Fox was planning to run for the presidency, which would involve going up against the powerful, entrenched Institutional Revolutionary Party, or PRI, that had controlled the Mexican presidency under single party-rule since 1929. Conventional wisdom said that nobody could successfully challenge the incumbent party machine. But Fox felt his National Action Party, proposing sweeping changes and reform, could prevail.

Among his goals were job creation and economic growth to better Mexico's suffering citizens, and a negotiated immigration accord with the United States. Lofty ambitions indeed, but Fox believed the nation had languished amid political corruption and hopeless inactivity for too long. He believed the people would support a visionary leader with values and principles they could trust.

Although I knew it was coming, I was still surprised when a year and a half after we first met, Fox again challenged me to participate full time in his presidential campaign. By this time I knew that arguing with him was futile, so I said yes. Although I had no political experience, I believed in his sincerity and vision. Without question, Mexico desperately needed the reforms and changes he was proposing.

I purposely declined to receive a salary, having no idea how I would support myself. My family and I just dropped everything, put my teaching and writing career on hold, and went to Mexico. It was almost a spiritual thing—somehow I knew it was what I was supposed to do.

At first, my main charge was to bring Mexicans in the United States into our movement to change Mexico. Fox would visit Dallas, Chicago, New York, and many other cities encouraging "paisanos" to call home and tell their family members to vote for a new Mexico. The excitement for "cambio" was evident among Mexican immigrants and Mexican-Americans as we rode horses through the streets of Chicago, spoke at packed stadiums during concerts of Mexican music stars Vicente Fernández or Los Tigres del Norte, and met with the leadership of Hispanic and Latin American organizations like La Raza, MALDEF, and LULAC.

I do not know if our strategy gave Fox a few hundred or many thousands of votes. But at the very least, our efforts created a great deal of public interest and awareness on both sides of the border.

Over the next three years, I performed a wide variety of tasks: providing counsel and advice on campaign communications and speeches, continuing to rally support from Mexican nationals working in the U.S., and serving as confidant, scheduler, and at times, unofficial chief of staff. My most notable job was exposing Fox and campaign leaders to U.S. American and European campaign "gurus" with innovative "foreign" ideas. Together we read dozens of books on how to run campaigns, and together we watched the U.S. presidential debates of Reagan, Kennedy, Nixon, and Clinton.

I brought in two key advisors—Dick Morris and Robert Allyn. Dick gave the green light on starting the campaign a thousand days before election day. And it was Dick—yes, Dick—who brought a strong spiritual emphasis to the campaign. He said, "I am a different Dick Morris. I no longer work for men but for God, and I want to help you and Mexico." And he did.

Robert Allyn participated for over two years in the campaign. He saw Fox through the debates and gave strategy ideas on days in which we were sure we were losing. He later created a "Democracy Watch" exit poll to make sure the world knew which candidate had won so no one could steal the election.

I could write volumes on the unselfish work Dick and Rob provided to the campaign. But that must be for another book.

In a sense, we had two types of campaigns going. One was intensely political, in which we carefully planned strategy for every step and avidly read every poll. The other was built on a deep faith that we were right and our opponents were wrong, and therefore, "fate," "providence"—"God" must be on our side.

Fox analyzed the numbers several times a day. We started with about eleven percent name recognition. This was not voter intent—just name recognition! Fox was a governor from a small state. His party, the PAN, did not support him very much at first. He was a Coca Cola executive, not much of a team player, not much of a politician. Fox did not win the primary of his party—he just became so popular that no one else in his party would run against him.

The first three fulltime campaign workers, Juan Antonio Fernández, Carlos Flores, and myself, spent many hours considering the moral and spiritual implications of the race. We were very much aware that we were participating in a very "spiritual" campaign. The PAN party openly promotes Catholic Christian values—Vicente Fox very openly prayed, went to mass, and asked Catholics and Protestants to pray for him.

Through the incredibly hectic campaign days, Carlos Flores somehow found time to go to mass every day. And I found myself saying short prayers before every strategy meeting and important campaign function. No one doubted that Fox needed divine protection.

During those grueling years of campaigning, from time to time in private moments together, Vicente would ask me questions about my Christian beliefs. He would say, "Come on, Juan, you're into something religious—tell me about it."

"No," I replied. "I'm not going to tell you."

"Well, are you Catholic?"

"Sure," I said.

"Are you Protestant?"

"Sure," I repeated.

"Andale, Juan, tell me the truth!"

I said, "I'm not going to let you pigeonhole me because then you won't listen to me."

I am sure that the best winning ideas for the campaign came from fellow campaign leaders like Eduardo Sojo (Vicente's closest economic adviser), Ramón Muñoz (the closest thing to a Chief of Staff in the presidency), Jorge Castañeda (the smartest of us all), Adolfo Aguilar Zinser (a true independent who helped Vicente better understand the left), el "Bigotón" González (the first campaign manager and the one who brought us all together), Paco Ortiz (the image and marketing guru of the campaign), Pedro Cerisola (the final campaign manager and day-to-day strategist), and P.A.N. party leaders such as Luis Felipe Bravo.

Nevertheless, since for many months I went everywhere with Vicente in Suburbans, buses, trains, helicopters, small planes, and on horses, he invariably got around to asking me for ideas — something new that could give us a few more points in the poll ratings. In turn I would mention an idea I had gotten from one of my gringo friends or my gringo readings. When Vicente asked me for a way to find more time in the day, I suggested he look at Bill Clinton's scheduling model. He did (and then made me his scheduler). When Vicente wanted new ideas on grassroots campaigning, I showed him what some of the campaign "textbooks" said. He agreed (and asked me to coordinate all logistics from then on). I stayed away from fundraising but brought in a Jewish lady that Dick Morris had recommended. Sheila Levin gave workshops to campaign fundraisers Lino Korrodi and Carlos Rojas.

Vicente never tired of hearing another one of my far-fetched suggestions. When some Mexican friends complained that my ideas were too American, Vicente always answered, "I don't care where the ideas come from. Ideas are not bad just because they come from another country. If they are bad, they are bad. If they are good, let's use them."

Having my ideas accepted was not always the best way to make friends. The person who fought me the most and supported me the most was the hardest working person in the campaign—Marta. If there is one person responsible for Vicente's victory it is Marta Sahagún, now Mrs. Fox.

"Juan changed my schedule. Juan says I cannot do another TV show. Juan..." And Vicente would interrupt—"You fight it out with Juan. He owns my time. Talk to him." Marta won much more than his time, of course. (Furthermore, she has won a special place in the history—and possibly the future—of Mexico.) Marta and I spent hundreds of hours arguing, strategizing, crying, and even praying.

My Personal Epiphany

Just as I had sought for a place in two countries, I also sought a solid religious ground. My father had been in the Catholic seminary—he claimed he was asked to leave because his rebellious spirit was not suitable clay for the priesthood. My mother, on the other hand, had "sought the God named Love" and had "found Christ" in a little Nazarene Church. So at the age of seventeen, one night on the rooftop of our Guanajuato home, I experimented with seeking God. The door I opened then has taken me on a path that still has not ended. It is a path in which faith is very important. I am a Christian, but titles and traditions have blurred in importance.

The presidential campaign was over on June 29, 2000, with three days of down time before the election on July 2. After months of hectic activity and with many people around at all hours of the day and night, everybody scattered. Early that morning it was just Vicente Fox, his personal aide named Felipe Zavala, a couple of guards, and me. We were driving between the Toluca airport and Mexico City when Fox asked if I was hungry. We stopped at a shack on the side of the road in a little town called La Marquesa.

We ordered some quesadillas and sat down. The guards went outside to wait, and Felipe got a phone call and walked away. So it was just the two of us, at the end of a thousand days of campaigning. And I distinctly felt it was important to pray.

"It's in God's Hands"

I said, "Well, Vicente, this campaign is over. I don't know what is going to happen, but we've done all we can do. If you're willing, I'd like for us to say a prayer right now and give this all to God. I want you to totally give yourself to Him—I mean everything, the whole campaign, your life, your plans—give it all to Him."

Vicente Fox looked me straight in the eyes and said, "I totally agree, let's do it!"

So sitting at a little lunch table in a rustic Mexican café, we held hands and he repeated a prayer after me. In no way am I suggesting that I "converted" Vicente Fox or exerted special influence upon him. I had known for a long time that he was a person who believed in and genuinely loved God. But this was a very special moment, I believe, for both of us.

For the next three days when anyone commented or asked about the election, he would simply repeat, "It's in God's hands! Right, Juan?"

July 2, 2000 was an historic date for Mexico, with probably the first truly democratic election in nearly a century. Against all odds, Vicente Fox and the PAN party won! Nobody thought he had a chance, but after seventy one years of one-party rule, the government was handed over to new leadership.

Vicente Fox gave his inaugural address, and as he came to the end of the speech, his children came up to him and handed him a large, two-foot cross. He lifted the cross high above his head—something that no one could remember ever being done in the history of Mexico. And he ended by saying, "God bless you!"

It was quite a testimony.

Following the election, President Fox asked Horacio McCoy, a highly respected Mexican "head-hunter" (and deeply spiritual man), to assist him in assembling the most qualified candidates in the world for potential appointment to his cabinet. Horacio sought out the most capable experts in the various areas of national responsibility, not only from within Mexico, but also expatriates from Europe, Asia, and other far-flung regions.

Fox then made his final selections from these candidates. Among other controversial appointments, I was asked to serve on the cabinet as Director of the Office of the President for Mexicans Abroad and Mexican Americans. Again breaking precedent, Vicente appointed a U.S. American to a Mexican cabinet position.

A Representative "of the People, for the People"

And so a boy from Texas found himself living in Mexico City, with an office in Los Pinos, the Mexican equivalent of the White House. My primary responsibility was to be a liaison between President Fox and the twenty-four million Mexicans and Mexican Americans living abroad, incorporating the needs of migrants and Mexican-Americans into his agenda. Fox and I had a running conversation about migrants. I commented on how much they suffered. He responded, "Yes, and look how much they have given to Mexico."

During my time in office, I fought to end border violence involving both the U.S. immigration officers and the "coyotes" who were unscrupulous opportunists who smuggled undocumented workers across the border for a price. If anything at all went wrong, it was always the poor who suffered, or in extreme cases, died.

I also led informational campaigns for the Mexican people on the dangers of border crossings, and sought understanding, respect, and recognition for those Vicente Fox calls Mexico's "heroes" working in the United States. These hard-working people sacrificed their lives and safety to make important contributions to the economy of their host country while sending hard-earned money back home to literally save their families from the ravages of hunger, sickness, and poverty.

In addition, I helped develop and establish programs such as the "Adopt a Community" program for the U.S.-Mexico Partnership for Prosperity, which sought capital investment for infrastructure and educational improvements in Mexico's poorest regions. Our goal was to find partners to help create and equip profitable enterprises that would allow Mexican workers to be gainfully employed at home. At the same time, these small businesses would learn to tap into Mexico's rich natural resources and export quality products to eager consumers abroad.

There was a very short honeymoon for the new Fox administration. Even the first hundred days were rough, with both the media and the "loyal" opposition being vicious in their attacks. Compounding the problem was the fact that many of the cabinet members, while unquestionable experts in their respective fields, had little or no experience in dealing with down-and-dirty partisan critics or the ruthlessness of the press. So the hassles were not long in coming. More than that, the inevitable infighting among those on our side also began to develop. It was frustrating, often heartbreaking, and exhausting. Nevertheless, we were advancing. There was still a feeling that Mexico was truly becoming a new Mexico.

Then Came September 11, 2001!

Overnight came a heightened awareness that the world had radically changed—and there would never be any going back to what used to be. A week earlier presidents Bush and Fox had met to discuss migration reform. The planned changes had to be set aside. The international economy, already in a slowdown, took a major

hit as a result of the terrorist crisis. A whole array of measures in-
tended to create more jobs in Mexico also was sidelined.

This made some of Fox's major campaign promises impossible to
bring about. Disappointing? Sure. But there has still been enormous progress in Mexico. The people wanted a real democracy,
and they got it. After seventy-one years of single-party rule, there
are now three strong parties in Congress. Those who have continued to offer bribes to government leadership have discovered that
they are not accepted by the Fox administration. And while many
have been disappointed with Fox's achievements, his virtual revolution is obvious everywhere you look. As Thomas Friedman, writing in an op-ed column for the New York Times, observed: "Because it happened so peacefully, it's easy to forget that Mexico in
one decade has gone through two remarkable revolutions. One of
the oldest one-party governments in the world was eased out with
ballots, not bullets, and a poor developing country lowered its tariff barriers and became America's second-largest trading partner."[1]

Democracy is not always neat and orderly, with steady progress as
planned. But change is underway…and must continue. That I, as a
Texas-born Mexican-American, was able to be an adviser to the
President of Mexico shows how far Mexico has come since I was a
child in Guanajuato. But it does not imply that we can allow the
important work of changing ideas about what it means to be a
Mexican to stop.

I resigned from working for Vicente Fox after about seven years to
return to Texas. Though he had offered me work for the entire six
years of his administration, I asked him to release me. It was not
that my commitment to helping improve the lives of Mexican immigrant workers had diminished—on the contrary, it is as strong as
ever. My goal of promoting understanding and cooperation between
the people of both countries is always on my mind; it is an all-
consuming passion, and it's the main reason I felt I must return to
the USA.

"Ye Shall Know the Truth..."

In today's U.S. America there is a vigorous emphasis on the controversial doctrine of separation of church and state. Yet not even the most radical secularist can honestly deny the fundamental influence of the Judeo-Christian ethic and basic biblical principles in laying the foundation and framing the structure of the government of the United States. The evidence may be found in the Constitution, the Bill of Rights, and numerous other national documents. The founders of our country were, to be sure, people of "the Book."

So it is interesting to note that both the Old and New Testaments forthrightly address the issue of immigrants, referring to them as "foreigners," "strangers" and "sojourners" (temporary residents) as well as the poor in dozens of verses. In "A Pastoral Letter Concerning Migration from the Catholic Bishops of Mexico and the United States," the authors point out biblical references such as in Leviticus, where Jehovah God said, "And if a stranger sojourns with you in your land, you shall not mistreat him. But the stranger who dwells among you shall be to you as one born among you, and you shall love him as yourself; for you were strangers in the land of Egypt" (Lev. 19:33-34).

In the New Testament, Jesus included the treatment of strangers in his teachings. He said, "I was hungry and you gave Me food; I was thirsty and you gave Me drink; I was a stranger and you took Me in" (Matthew 25:35, emphasis mine).

The righteous asked, "Lord, when did this happen?" And the response was, "...inasmuch as you did it to one of the least of these My brethren, you did it to Me" (Matthew 25:40).

While I certainly am not trying to preach a gospel of immigration, it seems to me that these, and numerous other biblical references, are undeniably relevant to immigration issues today.

Doing What is Right

With all my heart I believe there are ways to address the concerns of U.S. citizens about immigration. And there must be solutions that ensure fair, honest, and humane treatment of immigrant workers. If the present system is broken—and it is—let us employ the genius, wisdom, and imagination of U.S America to fix it. From the beginning of this nation, the passion of its citizens for freedom, justice, generosity, and fair play has made a place for immigrants from all over the world. U.S. America has always offered opportunities and helped harness the energies and talents of those who came for mutual benefit.

We need a comprehensive immigration reform. We need to find a way to dignify the millions who are already working here, enriching the U.S. We must also create a program that doesn't get us into trouble in the coming years. Though I supported the 1986-1987 amnesty, we should not have stopped there. We should have gone on to create a new immigration program that offered legal entry for needed workers. If we had done so, we would not have millions of undocumented today.

Immigrants often tell me, "It is easier to risk our lives walking through the hot deserts or climbing the cold mountains than to get legal papers!"

It is estimated that about 1.3 million Mexicans try to come across the border without papers every year. Without minimizing the fact that laws are broken, let me say that these are good people who simply want a job. These are desperate people who leave their families with tears in their eyes, knowing that this is their only chance to get food on the table, medicines for the mother, school books for the daughter, and tools for the brother.

About a million are caught trying to cross the line. About 300,000 make it into the U.S. They do not have a hard time finding jobs. They become the best of "citizens" of the U.S. as was proven by the amnesty of 1986-1987.

Let's fix the current laws, change the negative attitudes and practices that hurt us all, and create a workable, winning program that is good for both U.S. employers and immigrant workers...good for the United States...good for Mexico and other migrant sending nations. We should no longer say to the migrants, "Don't come, don't come...but if you will risk your life to cross the border, there is a great reward!"

And let us never forget that U.S.-Mexico cooperation is good for both countries for more than mere economic, ethical, or spiritual reasons. The United States and Mexico are "family," inextricably linked by history, proximity, and population. We share a 1,947 mile border on the same North American continent, as close to each other as the states of Virginia and Maryland, which surround Washington, D.C.

Mexicans already are an integral part of the U.S. society. For example, on my frequent trips to California, I am constantly reminded by teacher friends that sixty percent of children in that state are of Hispanic or Mexican descent. Sixty percent!

Already twenty-four million Mexicans or Mexican-Americans live in this great nation, and it is a prospering, vibrant country. Mexicans have been, and are, and will continue to be a part of that success. We love the United States! We can and will do great things for this nation in the future.

But Mexicans also want to see their parents' homeland south of the border grow, develop, and prosper. They would love for their children to be educated at home and have the opportunity to do important, fulfilling, profitable jobs in their own communities. Many would love to stay in Mexico in the warm circle of their own families and loved ones.

To do it, Mexico must work hard, but Mexico will prosper faster if it works with its friends. Mexicans are not just asking for a handout. They can and will pay their own way. Mexico is rich in culture, art, music, faith, and natural resources—but its real wealth is in its people. They will give their all if they have the opportunity.

Cooperation and sharing between the United States and Mexico is the only way to accomplish these goals so Mexico's dreams—and those of the United States—come true.

Throughout his campaign for re-election to a second term in office, George W. Bush pledged to continue to defend and protect the principles and values of the United States. He promised to keep making the hard decisions to do what is right—just because it is the right thing to do.

Following his victory in a hard fought election, political analysts, pollsters, and commentators agreed that his supporters rallied around the values Bush espoused and demonstrated. Values like morality, justice, freedom, and opportunity for all. These are values that U.S. citizens believe make living worthwhile, and are worth dying for! These are also values that immigrants passionately believe in and seek to practice freely, without fear.

The U.S. reaches out to Africa, and we should. We reach out to China, and that is good. We reach out to India, and Asia, and Europe, and many other territories, islands, and countries, and that is the way it should be.

But Mexico is our neighbor, our partner, our brother. We must first reach out to each other, then together open our arms to the world.

A very wise leader once said, "To truly know a man, you must first walk a mile in his shoes." This book seeks to bring greater understanding of our Mexican brothers and sisters living among us by analyzing the key issues in a balanced manner and presenting these new Americans and their heroic lives, as told in their own voices.

1 Thomas L. Friedman, "Out of the Box," New York Times, April 4, 2004.

Chapter 2

Mexico Is Our Friend, Our Partner, Our Family!

According to the headlines, sound bites, and TV talk shows, the United States is losing an ongoing battle to a fearsome, invading multitude of "dirty, dark, and dangerous" criminals intent on seizing the rich bounty of our prosperity and destroying the American way of life.

Yes, the Mexicans are coming! In fact, they're already here and are "burdening our country, taking our jobs, housing, and health care," some say.

Alarmist agitators like Colorado Congressman Tom Tancredo pander to uninformed citizens' fears and prejudices by warning that the U.S. is swimming in a sea of illegal aliens while national leaders ignore the destruction of the nation.[1] Is there no hope? Only, he says, if we begin rounding up and deporting the millions of Mexican and Central American "illegals," then militarize our border and use drones, sensors, radar, cameras and every other technological weapon available to keep them out. Finally, we must prosecute every U.S. employer who has ever hired an undocumented Mexican worker, he says.

Fox News Network's "fair and balanced" Bill O'Reilly repeatedly argues that the U.S. should line the border with battle ready troops[2] to stop any Mexican laborer who tries slipping over the line into the states...to get a job. Then, on a telecast in January, 2004, he mused, "Well, if I were only making $3500 a year and I could earn $35,000 across the border, maybe I'd cross that line, too!"

Two Latino journalists, Patrisia Gonzales and Roberto Rodriguez, writing in their *Albuquerque Journal* column on January 22, 2000, reported that, "Brazen anti-immigrant billboards and ads litter the country, particularly in Iowa, in attempts to poison the presidential election. It's hard to fathom seeing similar ads that target Whites, African-Americans or Jews."[3] Apparently the enemy Mexicans are fair game.

The Enemies of America

America does have enemies, and the nation has been under attack regularly for the last twenty-five years.

Somebody stormed the U.S. Embassy in Tehran, Iran and held all the American employees hostage in 1979. The enemy was not Mexico.

There were attacks on our embassy in Beirut, Lebanon, and on a Marine barracks in Beirut in 1983—but not by Mexico.

A Pan-American flight to New York was blown out of the sky over Lockerbie, Scotland in 1988. Mexico had nothing to do with it.

The first attack on the New York World Trade Center occurred in 1988—but not by Mexico.

The Khobar Tower military complex in Saudi Arabia was attacked in 1996, and two years later the U.S. Embassies in Kenya and Tanzania were targeted—none of them by Mexico.

An American warship, the USS Cole, was attacked in Aden, Yemen in 2000—but not by Mexico.

And on September 11, 2001, the Pentagon and the twin towers of New York's World Trade Center suffered catastrophic destruction and enormous loss of life when airliners were crashed into them—but not at the hands of Mexicans.

Who was responsible for these acts of war? Who is the enemy? The answers to these questions are important, but my point is, none of the attackers was a Mexican.

Yet, in the aftermath of the latest tragedy, would-be defenders from future violence look at the "wide open" 2,000 mile Mexican border and worry about how easy it would be for potential terrorists to cross. But no one can dispute the fact that none of the 9/11 attackers entered the U.S. from Mexico.

Is the Mexican Border a Threat?

An Associated Press report noted that U.S. officials said Mexican cooperation had been exemplary in addressing U.S. concerns about terrorists using the border as a transit point for attacks on U.S. soil. Both U.S. and Mexican authorities said they had taken significant steps to increase security along their shared border, but acknowledged it remained a "very attractive" route for terrorists wanting to do harm to the United States.[4]

Then how do we prevent potential terrorists from slipping across the border? According to some commentators, the answer is simple—just shut down and close the entire Mexican border. And before doing so, send all the Mexicans back home.

But wait! Mexico is not the enemy! Its good, honest, hard-working people provide a vast workforce estimated at eight million strong to power the U.S. economy, specializing in doing the jobs most Americans won't take, reported Jay Bookman in *The Atlanta Journal-Constitution* in a 2004 article. They pay taxes and social security—tens of billions of dollars annually—and get little or no benefits if they are undocumented. In 1999, employers paid $4.8 billion on $39 billion of earnings that the government can't match with actual persons, according to Mark Lassiter, a Social Security Administration spokesman. More recent estimates for social security payments to false names or accounts total as much as $7 billion.[5]

"That's money that the U.S. is absconding with because these workers will never get any benefit," said Eliseo Medina, an executive vice president with the Service Employees International Union.[6]

A 1997 study by the National Research Council questioned whether immigrants cost state and local governments more than they contribute in taxes or other economic benefits. The study cited state reports from California and New Jersey suggesting this was the case. However, James P. Smith, chairman of the panel that produced the report, believes the overall benefits from immigration outweigh the costs. "When immigrants come in, we as a nation gain from that," Smith said. "We win because our goods will be cheaper. Many more people will gain than lose."[7]

Daniel T. Griswold, an immigration expert at the Cato Institute in Washington, D.C., says, "Important sectors of our economy would be in deep trouble if they were deprived of their foreign-born workers, legal and illegal."[8]

Mexican migrant workers spend approximately eighty-five percent of their earnings in the local economy—as much as $85 billion annually, and the billions they send home each year have helped the Mexican government become the U.S.'s second largest trading partner.

Good workers. Good customers. Good neighbors.

More than twenty-five million individuals in the U.S. have family members in Mexico. Most Mexicans have at least one family member living in the U.S. Many living north of the border are directly affected by the Mexican economy, and virtually everybody in Mexico is affected by the ups and downs of the U.S. economy. So both countries have a stake in the success and well-being of the other.

How, then, did Mexico come to be regarded as such a threat? To understand, it is necessary to review a little history.

Writers Gonzales and Rodriguez point out that any Mexican or Central American person now living in the United States is already home, considering the ancient homeland of the indigenous people called Aztlán was somewhere in the American Southwest, according to all the ancient accounts.

How did We get Where We are Today?

The current U.S./Mexican border was established by the Treaty of Guadalupe Hidalgo in 1848. From then to 1929, Mexican immigrants freely crossed this newly established border. In fact, when the U.S. entered World War I, the government set up a recruitment program for Mexican workers. Between 1900 and 1930, about ten percent of Mexico's population—some 1.5 million people—emigrated to the United States.

Then came the Great Depression and a decade of joblessness, which led to a massive deportation campaign. In 1929, new laws passed made it a crime to enter the United States from Mexico without proper documentation. Mexicans still immigrated as they had before, except now they did so illegally.

In fact, the record shows that when it was convenient for the U.S. government to have cheap labor, strict immigration controls were relaxed without officially changing immigration law. For example, during World War II in the 1940's, the U.S. recruited Mexican labor to help farmers in crop production under the federal funded Bracero Program. Some five million Mexican immigrants were brought in and housed in government barracks, but with no worker benefits or union protection. And although sanctioned by the government, the Braceros were technically illegals according to the immigration laws.

This arrangement continued until the 1960's, by which time millions of Mexicans had acquired the expertise to migrate on their own. According to Princeton professor Douglas S. Massey, "From 1965 to 1985, undocumented migration to the United States fluctuated with the rhythms of the Mexican and American economies and increased at a slow but steady pace. But despite alarmist rhetoric, the border was never 'out of control.'"[9]

Massey, co-author of *Beyond Smoke and Mirrors: Mexican Immigration in an Age of Economic Integration*, notes that most immigrants came to the U.S. because of economic problems at home. Once they earned enough to provide for their families, and to finance homes, products, and sometimes businesses, about eighty-five percent of those who entered the country ultimately went back home.

So what happened to get us where we are today? Massey says that beginning in 1986, the U.S. adopted "a schizophrenic policy toward Mexico. On the one hand, Washington sought to create an integrated North American market with free movement for goods, capital, information, and services. On the other hand, the United States devoted more time and money to prevent the movement of labor."

The increased border management policy didn't work. The rate of entry of undocumented immigrants continued to climb. David Brooks of *The New York Times* observed that most illegal immigrants are so desperate to provide for their families that they will "wade across rivers, brave 120 degree boxcars, and face vicious smugglers" for the chance at a better life.[10] But the tightened restrictions did make it more difficult—and dangerous—to risk going back home. So most of them didn't leave. Instead, they tried to get family members from Mexico to join them. New people kept coming, so the total number of immigrants inside the country soared.

The result has been that what once was a natural circular movement of workers coming to the U.S. and going back to Mexico has changed into a settled population of dependents.

The Unwritten "Understandings"

For decades Mexico and the United States have had an unwritten understanding, a perfect situation for everyone except the immigrants. Officially, the U.S. said, "Don't come, don't come—but if you make it we'll put you to work. We'll let you pay social security and taxes, but we won't have to give you any worker benefits. You can do the jobs our workers don't care about. Then, if we ever want you out, we can just send you home."

Mexico said, "Well, let the people go. We can't provide work for them, so this is a great escape valve. And they'll send money to take care of their families that we don't have to give. Hopefully things will get better someday and they can come back home."

On one of my frequent visits to the "line," I saw several U.S. border officials inspecting the barbed wire fence close to a small town in Arizona. I called out a greeting and walked over to them...from the Mexican side.

Their body language was tense, saying "Don't get too close!" Then they seemed to notice that I was very relaxed and looked like an "Anglo." I asked them in English how they were doing on such a hot summer day.

They hesitantly returned the greeting. With both of my feet still in Mexico, I told them I was a U.S. citizen working with President Fox on immigration issues. They were not impressed, but one of the three officers seemed to recognize me from a recent *Nightline* interview. I assured them that I was just looking at the conditions of the border and wondered how many had died there this summer.

"About one a day," one of them volunteered.

"That's terrible," I said and then mumbled, "sure seems unfair." I got a lot of mumbled comments back.

One man said, "It is all so different down here from what Washington and Mexico City think."

I agreed and then asked, "What do you do about it?"

"Well, I try to inform them as much as I can..."

Another officer spoke, "They know when we need workers..."

"Yeah," said the third border officer. "We get orders to 'Open the faucet...look the other way.' Then they say, 'Close the faucet.' We just do it."

Concerned people on both sides of the immigrant issue agree that many of the migrants would prefer a circular migration, coming to the U.S. to work for a time, then returning to their families in Mexico. To that end, President Bush has proposed granting work permits and temporary legal status to millions of migrants who now live in the U.S. illegally. Under the plan, undocumented workers—mainly from Mexico—could obtain three-year renewable work visas with full employee benefits and legal protection.

All those with work visas could enter and exit the country freely, without worrying about being barred from reentry. By documenting these millions, not only could the U.S. gain better control of its borders, but also newly documented migrants would be free to return home and contribute to Mexico's development.

While the Bush proposal will go through much discussion and negotiations, one positive is that the visa offer represents a change in attitude toward migrant workers. American law—and American public opinion—have long treated these workers as "criminals." Bush's proposal recognizes that these Mexicans are "honest people, working hard for a better life."

Can Our Continent Become a Community?

There are many who say this program does not go far enough in dignifying the millions of Mexican people who are already here. They believe these undocumented residents should be given citizenship—or at least placed on a "good citizenship track" to full recognition. I agree that the present system is broken and must be fixed.

For example, Professor Massey stresses we should expand the legal quota for Mexican immigration. "The current limit of 20,000 permanent resident visas per year for a peaceful border country of 105 million linked to the United States by treaty is ridiculously small," he says. With waiting lists of thousands, and an average processing time measured in years, the present immigration policy is obviously inadequate and unrealistic.

The existing system offers the worst of all possible worlds, says Massey, "massive in-migration, little out-migration, and the accumulation of a costly, marginalized population north of the border."[11] By taking some decisive steps, we have the opportunity to create a circular migration for those who want it, lower the costs of immigration (if, in fact, it is true that there are great costs), and boost economic growth and development in Mexico.

Texas Senator John Cornyn said in a recent Senate Judiciary Committee hearing, "For far too long, the debate over immigration has divided Americans of good will into one of two camps—those who are angry and frustrated by our failure to enforce the rule of law, and those who are angry and frustrated that our immigration laws do not reflect reality. But both camps are right."[12]

A bi-partisan bill introduced by Senator John McCain and Senator Ted Kennedy in May, 2005, discusses a step toward addressing these concerns. The proposal offers a more realistic guest worker visa program of up to 400,000 per year, as well as a plan for undocumented workers already in the country to get "legal" and start on the process for permanent legal status.

Most importantly, we must find a way to stop seeing our neighbors to the south as enemies. Mexico is not the enemy. Mexicans are loving, generous people who only need opportunity to receive as much as they contribute. So we must learn to be partners.

Dr. Jim Turpin, founder of the international humanitarian organization, Project Concern, once said, "We must stop trying to be our brother's keeper and instead become our brother's…brother."[13]

We live on the same continent—Canada, the United States, and Mexico. We must find ways to cooperate and work together as the North American Community! I have frequently been criticized for supposedly promoting a no-border policy for these neighbor nations. I do not promote a no-border policy, but I do recognize that the economic world is changing rapidly, and more and more nations are jostling to compete in international trade.

The day will come—I believe in twenty-five years or less—when Canada, the United States, and Mexico will find it necessary—imperative—to share their unique, vital assets and work together as a block, (not one country), to compete with the European block,

China, Japan and other emerging economic powers. It is now, and increasingly will be, advantageous for each North American neighbor to recognize that we are friends, partners, and family!

1 John Hawkins, "An Interview with Congressman Tom Tancredo (R-CO)," rightwingnews.com, January 28, 2003.

2 Bill O'Reilly, "The O'Reilly Factor," FoxNews.com, January 23, 2002.

3 Patrisia Gonzales and Roberto Rodriguez, Column of the Americas, "Going back to where we came from," *Albuquerque Journal*, January 22, 2000.

4 George Gedda, *Associated Press*, November 10, 2004.

5 Katherine Reynolds Lewis, "Do immigrants really take jobs Americans don't want?" Newhouse News Service, January 2004.

6 Ibid.

7 National Research Council, "The New Americans: Economic, Demographic, and Fiscal Effects of Immigration (James P. Smith and Barry Edmonston, editors, 1997).

8 "Immigration," Cato Handbook on Policy, Cato Institute, Washington, D.C., December 8, 2004.

9 Douglas S. Massey, "Mexican migrants need to find a way to go home," *The Los Angeles Times*, November 25, 2004.

10 David Brooks, "Workers in the Shadows," Op-Ed column, *The New York Times*, January 2004.

11 Massey, *The Los Angeles Times*, November 25, 2004.

12 Paul Barton, "Proposal for aliens draws ire of many," Arkansas Democrat-Gazette, June 19, 2005, p. 14A.

13 Dr. James W. Turpin with Al Hirshberg, *A Faraway Country—The Continuing Story of Project Concern* (New York: The World Publishing Company, 1970).

Chapter 3

Un Día Sin Mexicanos

Prior to the U.S. presidential election of 2004, an independent Mexican film company produced a quirky movie called "Un Día Sin Mexicanos" (A Day Without A Mexican). Described as "a comedic commentary on America's attitudes toward its largest minority group," the movie envisions what might happen if somehow all the Mexican immigrants in California suddenly disappeared. The resulting chaos soon propels the regular citizens left behind to quickly realize the value of immigrant workers as well as their contributions to the state's welfare, and to plead for their return. Then, *poof*, the Mexicans are back, receiving cheers, adulation, and new appreciation from everybody.[1]

The movie's outlook may be too simplistic; (and may have unnecessary sexual overtones, as some have complained). Nevertheless, it does address some of the mistaken attitudes and opinions of increasingly vocal critics and opponents of Mexican migrant workers. There are many valid facts and issues that no longer can be overlooked, willfully ignored, or deliberately misrepresented.

Columnist and commentator George Putnam has described Mexican immigration as an "illegal alien invasion…a nation-destroying dilemma not known since the Roman Empire fell before the marauding vandals." He declares that the U.S. is "facing an out-and-out conspiracy against every citizen, and the invasion continues."[2]

Colorado Congressman Tom Tancredo demands that all employers who hire illegal Mexican workers should be prosecuted to the full extent of the law. "If we, in fact, were to begin enforcing the law against people who are hiring people who are here illegally," he said, "then you would find that many of the millions of people who are here would go back home." Then, he says, all "illegal aliens" can and should be rounded up and "we could begin deporting—and yes, I mean deporting."[3] He also accuses President Bush of "ignoring the destruction of the nation" by seeking to reform U.S. immigration laws, because the proposed temporary worker program is, in Bush's words, "more rational and more humane."[4] Bill O'Reilly of Fox News Network also proposes stationing battle-ready U.S. troops on the Mexican border, along with "predators" to seal the border.[5] "They should seal it," he says, "because that would stop the chaos."[6]

In an interview with Univision TV anchorman Jorge Ramos, O'Reilly spoke of "millions coming across the Mexican border, a lot of them with drugs." He said "there's a lot of bad guys coming over" and that "twenty-five percent of all the people incarcerated in California are illegal immigrants...that's criminals!"[7]

Do these outspoken critics of immigration reform honestly believe that the undocumented immigrants hired by U.S. American companies and citizens to do jobs other workers won't do are drug-smuggling criminals and "marauding vandals?" Could it be true that pro-immigration reform Democrats and Republicans along with hard-working Mexicans sending financial support home to desperately needy families are actually part of a conspiracy to destroy the nation and "every citizen" of the U.S.?

A brief review of world history recalls that the Vandals were vicious barbarians who attacked defenseless villages, raping and pillaging, burning homes and fields, killing all inhabitants, and leaving only scorched earth in their wake. Have you heard of any towns and people being ravaged by vicious Mexicans? Or what about drug smuggling? No. For the most part, migrant workers usually only do the dirty, dangerous tasks U.S. Americans don't want to do.

As to the "criminals" in California jails—how many of the alleged "twenty-five percent" were convicted of "crimes" like driving without a license and/or without insurance (which they could not obtain without documentation). Yes, a combination of those types of offenses can result in both large fines *and* jail time for immigrants.

The 21ˢᵗ Century Great Exodus

Suppose the viewpoint of critics like Tom Tancredo became official U.S. policy and it actually was possible for all undocumented Hispanic migrant workers to be rounded up and deported. (As one Anglo character in the "Un Día Sin Mexicanos" movie offensively put it, "All the Mexicans are gone—even the ones from El Salvador, Argentina, and Spain.")

Would we notice their absence ABSOLUTELY! Immediately the chaos the movie imagined for California would become desperate reality for the entire nation. The explosive result would have one of the most disruptive negative impacts on daily living in the history of the United States.

U.S. American agriculture would be dealt a virtual deathblow. Farms and orchards would lose the workers who plant the crops, tend the plants, and gather the harvest. Domestically grown vegetables and strawberries would rot in the fields. U.S. crops of apples, pears, oranges, grapefruits, peaches, apricots—and everything else—would be wasted for lack of pickers. Shipments of produce to markets would stop.

U.S. meat packers and poultry processors would shut down, since the majority of their plants are manned by immigrant labor. Many company presidents have personally told me that they would find it almost impossible to open the doors to their plants without Mexican immigrant workers. Their industry welcomes a realistic and regulated guest worker program that provides essential labor and guaranteed genuine benefits to both migrant workers and U.S. employers. Furthermore, most would support an immigration bill that would give these immigrants an eventual open door to U.S. citizenship.

Un día sin Mexicanos? Imagine what would happen to restaurants. Without Mexican low paid workers, who would deliver and stock the raw ingredients and foodstuffs for the daily menu? Who would prepare the food, serve it, clear the tables, and wash the dishes?

The same is true for hotels and motels. Mexican migrant labor drives the vans and buses, handles guests' luggage, cleans the rooms, launders the linens and towels, and maintains the buildings.

An enormous crisis would occur in the nation's hospitals, nursing homes, and child care centers. A significant percentage of the professional and medical staff would be gone, along with virtually all those in support jobs. Many hospitals would be reduced to emergency room services only. Many nursing homes and childcare centers simply could not open their doors.

Both public and private schools would lose vital staff. In some areas, as many as twenty percent of the teaching faculty are Hispanic...some of them are undocumented. An even greater percentage of food service, janitorial and other support service staff would be permanently absent.

Overnight, the home-building and general construction industries nationwide would have only skeleton crews. Even smaller home repair companies would drastically downsize or shut down. How prevalent is Mexican labor in the industry? Enormous! For example, did you realize that many of the construction workers who rebuilt the Pentagon after the 9/11 attack were Mexican and Central American immigrants?

There's almost no end to the businesses and industries that would be crippled or at least severely pinched by the loss of Mexican labor. The list is mind-boggling—retail sales, domestic services, landscaping/lawncare companies, municipal water and sewage systems, textile factories and other light manufacturing, transportation, the moving business, railroad yards, the warehouse industry, etc. Did you know that a whopping eighty-four percent of forestry workers are Hispanic? Who would do all these jobs if the immigrant labor force were deported?

Even before such drastic action as deporting all undocumented migrants, there is already a lack of unskilled employees in many areas. The highly respected Pew Hispanic Center (funded by the Pew Charitable Trusts of Philadelphia), notes that "the U.S. economy has an appetite and even a need for more workers than are available legally." Its studies suggest the need is more in the range of a million plus per year.[8] Yet, according to a policy report by the Cato Institute, "U.S. immigration law provides no legal channels through which low-skilled foreign-born workers can enter the United States to fill the growing gap between demand and supply...."[9]

What Happens Next?

Suppose for the sake of argument that following a mass deportation, the government was able to line up all able-bodied workers on welfare rolls and unemployment lists and press them into service, along with the relatively small number of new legal "green card" immigrants coming into the country each year. The added expense of providing these new U.S. workers at least minimum wages, overtime pay, healthcare insurance, and safe working conditions would instantaneously drive up the cost of labor by an estimated twenty-five to fifty percent. These increased overhead expenses could not be absorbed by employers and would be passed on to the U.S. consumer in price increases or added fees.

But in reality there are not enough native-born workers or legal immigrants available to replace all the deportees. That being fact, inevitably many enterprises would not be able to stay in business, and fewer services would be provided. For example, the housing, shops, and other businesses that had catered to the now-missing low income undocumented workers would be forced to shut down.

According to the Mexican government, *paisanos* in the U.S. now sent home close to $20 billion annually (approximately ten to fifteen percent of their earnings) to help provide a better life for their extended families.[10] The total of these "remittances" is approximately two-thirds as much as the production of Pemex, the state-

owned petroleum industry, which is the nation's top revenue pro-
ducer. Combined with the rest of Mexico's gross national product,
the spendable funds available catapulted the nation to the position of the U.S.'s second largest economic partner.

Of course, the loss of income from workers deported from the U.S.
(who would now be unemployed in Mexico) would cause that level
of trade to plummet.

But this wouldn't be the only financial loss to the U.S. As mentioned, undocumented Mexican workers send only fifteen percent
or less of their earnings back home—usually about $350 per month.
The rest of their income, a combined total of some $84 billion, is
spent in the United States—for taxes, other withheld contributions, and on food, rent and utilities, transportation, entertainment,
and other basic living expenses. Of course, after a mass deportation, that entire economy would come to a screeching halt.

According to a National Immigration Forum study published by
the Cato Institute, undocumented immigrants pay about $7 bil-
lion annually in taxes, including $2.7 billion a year to Social Secu-
rity, and $168 million into state unemployment benefit funds. By
law, they cannot collect any benefits for these contributions, so
they amount to direct subsidies. As a result, immigration actually
improves the finances of the two largest federal income transfer
programs, Social Security and Medicare.[11]

In the state of California alone, which may account for more than
forty percent of the undocumented population, immigrant workers
pay an additional $732 million in state and local taxes. Basically,
the only benefits the workers receive in return are education for
their children and emergency medical care.

David Bacon, a specialist in international labor issues, writes, "It is
difficult to make the case that expenditures on the education of
undocumented children, or on emergency medical care for their
families, is a net economic drain, given the gross overpayment of
benefits in many other areas."[12]

So, Let's do the Math...

According to the Cato Handbook on Policy, there were an estimated eight to ten million people living in the United States without documents as of 2004. What do you think the dollar cost would be to gather all of the Mexican citizens and transport them to the border? It would amount to billions of dollars, and who would be responsible for carrying out this logistical nightmare? What would the humanitarian cost be—to the immigrants, to their children (some of whom are U.S. citizens—do they go or stay?), and to the millions of extended families in Mexico who are dependent on their loved one's monthly remittances from the U.S.?

What happens to the houses, mobile homes, furniture, cars, and other possessions owned or being paid for monthly by a great many undocumented immigrants?

What toll would the deportation take on U.S. businesses and individual citizens who need low cost Mexican labor to survive? How many small businesses would shut down? Realistically, what impact would this forced exodus of a vital work force have on the health and growth of the U.S. economy?

Perhaps the sum total of all these considerations is still not the greatest cost—or loss—a mass deportation would bring to U.S. America. President George W. Bush, in a January 2004 speech proposing a new and sweeping reform of the nation's immigration policies, referred to certain other invaluable and irreplaceable contributions of Mexican immigrants. He said:

"America is a stronger and better nation because of the hard work and the faith and the entrepreneurial spirit of immigrants... One of the primary reasons America became a great power in the twentieth century is because we welcomed the talent and the character and the patriotism of immigrant families...

"As a Texan, I have known many immigrant families, mainly from Mexico, and I've seen what they add to our country. They bring to America the values of faith in God, love of family, hard work, and self-reliance; the values that made us a great nation to begin with."

What price do we place on those values? Can we afford to reject those who offer such treasured gifts and cruelly trample their living contributions underfoot? Surely that is a cost too great for any true American citizen to ever even consider.

If the System is Broken, Let's Fix It!

Undoubtedly there are some fundamental problems and inequities with our current immigration system. Let us recognize the reality and the benefits of Mexican migration to the United States. Our present policies regarding guest workers are totally unrealistic and out of touch. An employment system that requires the utilization of ten million undocumented workers winks at the law and invites abuses.

As President Bush noted in his speech proposing reforms to the present U.S. immigration system, "Workers who seek only to earn a living end up in the shadows of American life, fearful, often abused and exploited. When they're victimized by crimes they're afraid to call the police or seek recourse in the legal system. They are cut off from their families far away, fearing if they leave our country to visit relatives back home they might never be able to return to their jobs. The situation I described is wrong. It is not the American way."[13]

One key element of a more sensible border policy would be a temporary visa system allowing workers from Mexico and other countries to work in the U.S. for a fixed time. The policy would also match willing guest workers with willing U.S. employers who have jobs they cannot fill.

Under the new policy, immigrant workers would be protected by labor laws, with the right to change jobs, earn fair wages, and have the same working conditions the law requires for U.S. American workers. It would also guarantee their right to report grievances without fear of reprisal.

Being "documented" would also allow them to establish legal identification documents, and to freely pass back and forth across the border. This expanded and orderly visa program ultimately would reduce the number of permanent Mexican residents by encouraging a return to the natural circular migratory flow.

Another crucial element of real immigration reform would allow undocumented workers already in the country to become legal. This would encourage millions of people now living in the shadows to make themselves known to authorities by registering with the government without fear of deportation.

Some temporary workers would certainly decide to seek American citizenship. Many legislators—both Democrats and Republicans—acknowledge that the citizenship line is too long, and the current limits on legal immigration are too low. These issues can and should be addressed to find solutions that are mutually beneficial. But no matter how small the window of opportunity, there should be—there must be—some light at the end of the tunnel for those seeking citizenship.

The best long-term solution to illegal immigration from Mexico is sustained growth south of the border to create opportunities and security at home for Mexican workers. There must be ways the United States can assist in expanding economic opportunity for our next door neighbor on the continent.

Conservative columnist Bruce Walker notes that "Mexico is one of the great lost opportunities of our times." With a little more than a third of the U.S. population and about a third of the U.S.'s physical size, if Mexico's economy operated at the same level of per capita GDP as our economy, "then Mexico would have the fourth largest economy in the world, after only America, China, and Japan. In a few years, given demographic trends, it would be the third largest economy in the world. That is a breathtaking prospect, and there is no reason why it cannot become a reality."[14]

I believe there are good, honorable answers and solutions to the problems and challenges before us. We will explore some of the possibilities at greater length. With all my heart I believe there is a way that will bless everybody involved if we will work together to find it.

1 Daniel McGroarty (White House Writers Group, Washington, D.C.), "Isolating, and dealing with, the 'L Factor,'" *Tulsa World*, August 22, 2004, p. G3.

2 "One Reporter's Opinion—Illegal Alien Problem Mainstream at Last!", NewsMax.com, October 2, 2004.

3 "An Interview with Congressman Tom Tancredo (R-CO)" by John Hawkins, rightwingnews.com, July 28, 2003.

4 Ibid.

5 John Hawkins, "An Interview with Congressman Tom Tancredo," rightwingnews.com, July 28, 2003.

6 "The O'Reilly Factor," foxnews.com, January 23, 2002.

7 Univision Anchor Jorge Ramos, "The O'Reilly Factor," foxnews.com, January 23, 2002.

8 "Survey of Mexican Migrants," Trends 2005, The Pew Research Center, Washington, D.C., January 24, 2005.

9 "Immigration," Cato Handbook on Policy, Cato Institute, Washington, D.C., December 8, 2004.

10 "Mexican Remittances Exceed $14.5 billion," mixicosolidarity.org/news, October 27, 2003.

11 Op cit.

12 David Bacon, "An Immigration Policy Based on Human Rights," dbacon.igc.org, (Institute for Global Communications), February 2, 1998.

13 President George W. Bush, speech proposing new temporary worker program and immigration policy reform, January 7, 2004.

14 Bruce Walker, "How President Bush will transform the world," enterstageright.com/archive/articles/1000presidentbush, October 16, 2000.

Chapter 4

Meet Your New Neighbors —
Hearing the New Voices of America

I traveled to the United States every week during the first year and a half in my post as Special Advisor for Mexicans Abroad to President Vicente Fox. On these trips, which took me frequently to Texas, California, and Illinois, but also to Nebraska, Alaska, and North Carolina, I had the privilege of meeting the Mexican migrants who have sacrificed everything to go north so their families can have a better life.

I met entrepreneurs who made it big…and senior citizens who have little to show financially for their time in the United States. I met undocumented high school students praying for the chance to attend college…and Mexican-born U.S. citizens who now hold public office. I met enthusiastic new citizens eager to fulfill their own American dream in this country…and homesick migrants whose only dream is to earn enough to go home to Mexico.

As each person told me his or her story, I wished that I could share its vividness with others—with those who support immigrants and immigration reform and those who don't. I knew these stories needed to be heard by Native Americans, Mexicans, Mexican-Americans, and by the children and grandchildren of previous immigrant generations. These voices need to be heard by African-Americans, Asian Americans, Irish-Americans, Polish-Americans, and Jewish-Americans.

If only everyone could hear these stories, I thought, we might be able to change the debate from talking about "immigration" to talking about immigrants. We would talk about the real people, the good people who have made life as we know it possible—both for U.S. Americans and for Mexicans.

I want you to hear the new voices of this great country and to get acquainted with your new neighbors. The people in this book are not meant to be "representative" of the Mexican immigrant experience, at least not in any scientific way. In fact, the opposite is true. I have chosen them precisely because they break so many of the "rules" of immigrant storytelling

In all cases, undocumented immigrants have disguised their names, and legal immigrants were given the opportunity to do so as well. Names of towns, workplaces, churches, friends, and family members have been changed.

While many undocumented immigrants live in constant fear, this fear need not—and does not—paralyze or silence them. Those immigrants, whose status became legal in the amnesty that accompanied the 1986 Immigration Reform and Control Act, spoke openly of their life histories, both the documented and undocumented parts.

The majority of the interviews for this book were conducted in Spanish, though rare was the interviewee who did not throw in an English word or two. Likewise, a few interviews took place in English, but almost never without some Spanish interspersed. It two noteworthy cases, the interview was conducted in Spanish, although this was the second language of the indigenous Mexican interviewees.

My collaborator in gathering this mixed choir of voices, and then editing and translating, is Julie Weise, the great-granddaughter of Russian and Polish Jewish immigrants to the United States. She brought to our discussions of immigrant narrative the memories of her family, passed on to her by her great-grandmother, Esther Giberman. The commonalities and tensions in our understanding of what it means to belong to two nations at once influence the way in which these stories are told.

Stories Are for Telling

I have selected seven aspects of the immigrant "story" to explore. Some of these themes, like "Down to Business," which focuses on Mexican immigrants who start small businesses, fit squarely into popular conceptions of how immigrants have made the United States their own. Others, like "Still in Mexico," profile Mexicans who continue investing themselves in Mexico even after decades in the U.S.; these directly challenge popular perception.

My hope is that these oral accounts will draw attention to stories emerging from the new meeting points of Mexico and the United States, which are just beginning to attract the attention of researchers. In the past decade, thousands of indigenous Mexicans have come to the United States. Their stories are included along with those of immigrants from traditional migrant-sending states like my Guanajuato. Many indigenous migrants arrive speaking Zapoteco or Mixteco rather than Spanish, and some might say they "become Mexican" by spending time with other Mexican immigrants north of the border.

The other new points of meeting are the small towns in the South and Midwest that have seen their Mexican populations go from zero to several thousand within a decade. Mexican immigrant pioneers no longer limit themselves to Los Angeles, Houston, or Chicago when they decide where to move. They seek opportunities and follow family to other places where their labor is urgently needed. Six of the nation's fastest-growing Mexican communities are in the state of North Carolina. From Alaska to Georgia, they're turning cities and towns throughout the United States into my parents' kitchen—places where Mexico and the U.S. encounter one another.

As a Mexican-American, I also see the urgent need to challenge Mexico's idea of its own history and culture. Today, Mexico is a nation of about 129 million people—105 million in Mexico and 24 million in the United States. The Mexican immigrants profiled in this book along with their U.S.-born children and grandchildren, must also be written into Mexican history as bearers of a pioneering tradition—that of crossing the border to help feed their families. The classmates who thought that I, as a Mexican-American in Guanajuato, was an outsider were right and wrong.

What is the meaning of the Mexican immigrant experience? What do the oral histories in this section of the book say about the future of the hemisphere? As you will see, the best storytellers are the migrants themselves—and the first to speak is a young woman from a town called Mexico.

A Note On Translation

My background is in poetry and literary translation, Julie's is in anthropology. Together we have considered that the work of translating these immigrants' words into English is one of the most challenging aspects of writing this book. We have sought to retain the essence of the interviewee's way of speaking, even as we acknowledge that such an attempt to capture these "natural" patterns can have the effect of putting the immigrant at a linguistic disadvantage. Indeed, we believe colloquial phrases sound "less educated" in print than they do verbally. We write with only the utmost respect for the dignity and intelligence of these interviewees, and believe that the best way to demonstrate this is to retain as many sparks of individuality and humanity as possible in our translation between them and you.

Part 1:

Firsts

Seven-year-old Sandra and three-year-old Carlos were about to start school in Mexico, and the school had sent a representative to teach them a few key phrases so they could get by in a classroom where no one would speak their language. "I have to go to the bathroom," practiced the brother and sister over and over.

They knew they would have each other, but only each other. Carlos and Sandra nervously prepared to enter a classroom in which everything would be foreign to them.

Holding hands, they approached the school doors. Sandra and Carlos were about to become the first foreigners at school in rural Mexico…

…that is, Mexico, Missouri.

Becoming American

I begin with the story of Sandra because, in some ways, it reminds me of so many first days of school that I experienced moving between Guanajuato and Texas when I was young. I am not alone in this. Understanding how it feels to be the newcomer, it seems, is a shared experience that defines being a foreigner, as well as an American.

Nonetheless, some might say Sandra and her family are *un*-American. They still speak Spanish at home, they dream of returning to Mexico, and they are in the United States without legal papers.

Most U.S. Americans I know tend to be proud that their forebears came from somewhere else. Their parents or great-great grandparents, the story goes, were enterprising newcomers who came looking to start a new life in the United States, escaping poverty or strife in their home countries. Stepping off the proverbial boat, their first years were marked with destitution and struggle. Yet they had a determination to get ahead, to learn English, and to "become American" culturally.

Some say yesterday's newcomers do not have anything to do with today's primarily non-white immigrants. There are two key ways the experience of the Mexican recent arrivals—like Sandra and her family—purportedly differ from that of their earlier counterparts in other immigrant groups. First, the reasoning goes, while other immigrants came to the United States with the intention of staying "for good," the Mexican arrives with a different plan—a temporary stay to acquire a bit of savings and then return to the home country. As a result, Mexican immigrants are less interested in learning English and in "becoming American."

Second, many argue that the sheer volume and endless incoming flow has made these immigrants "unabsorbable" since keeping to their own communities becomes too easy. Once again, this is seen as contributing to the lack of "Americanization" among Mexican immigrants.

Critics have many of their facts straight. But if they listened, as I have, to today's Mexican immigrants tell their stories, they might see that these facts do not imply that Mexican immigrants are "un-American"—but rather, the opposite is true.

Arriving with plans to return is, in fact, a hallmark of migration from the family-oriented Mexican culture. The people in this chapter, Sandra, Miguel, Lucía and Rodrigo, all dream of going back to Mexico one day.

Yet, they already have begun to build a life in the United States, developing a connection to their new country and coming to share values and experiences with their neighbors.

The presence of some twenty-five million Mexicans and Mexican-Americans in the United States attests that today's temporary migrants are tomorrow's permanent migrants. Mexicans are hardly the first group of "new" immigrants who initially arrived with a desire to return home, nor are they the first to find their stays lengthening and their families becoming a part of American society.

For example, observers of Italian immigration in the early twentieth century noted that Italian immigrants "carry their mother country in their hearts and maintain a political tie with it…they return as soon as they have put together a small nest egg. In this respect they are different from the English, Irish and Germans who go to America to become citizens." In some years, there were an average of seventy three Italians returning to Italy for every one hundred that came to the U.S.[1]

But the end of the story is well known in the cultural and political history of the United States. Many Italians did end up staying, and they made their mark on the nation. Even as Sandra, José, Lucía and Rodrigo dream of a future in the land of their birth, these immigrants are laying the foundations for Missourian, Carolinian, Californian, and Iowan lives.

Their experience has been more common—in fact, has been the norm—since redoubled border patrol efforts in 1994 and 2001.

While crossing the border illegally was once as simple as waiting until dark and running across the line, in recent years it has become an expensive and life-threatening ordeal. Smugglers, or "coyotes," charge thousands of dollars to lead migrants across, and hundreds lose their lives each year on the journey. So Mexicans in the United States lengthen their stays and bring their families north rather than return to Mexico for a visit with the knowledge that getting back would require them to make the grueling and dangerous crossing again. Migration patterns that once looked like a circle today look more like a straight line to permanent settlement in the United States.

But, do these Mexican immigrants care as much about becoming American as Irish and Italian immigrants did? With so many Mexican immigrants in the United States, don't they stay linguistically and culturally "in Mexico" even if they physically reside in Los Angeles, Houston, or Chicago?

Vibrant Mexican communities indeed thrive in parts of these and other big cities, as well as in rural areas of California and Texas. But the immigrant stories in this chapter demonstrate a different reality — one I have seen on countless visits all over the nation. Today, hundreds of thousands of Mexican immigrants have chosen to pioneer new territory—to go to North Carolina or Iowa, rather than compete with hundreds of thousands of other Mexicans for jobs in cities like San Diego, Dallas, and New York. The lower cost of living in these smaller towns and Southern cities also draws immigrant families to settle down.

Far from the bilingual classrooms of California, today Sandra is one of just a dozen Mexican children in Mexico, Missouri's elementary school. Rodrigo is trying to organize one of the first community groups in Charlotte, North Carolina. And Miguel enjoys the small-town life of Red Oak, Iowa, where he is the first Mexican homeowner and the first Mexican family on his block.

Does living in an ethnic enclave without legal working papers hinder the development of an American identity among Mexican immigrants? Not in Lucía's case. Even she, who has settled among hundreds of thousands of farm workers in a ninety- percent-Hispanic part of California's Central Valley and dreams vividly of a return to Mexico, realized after the attacks on the World Trade Center just how much a part of the United States she already feels.

Sandra, the Pioneer

Listening to eight-year-old Sandra tell the story of her first day of school in near-perfect English, it is hard to believe the day occurred just one year ago.

> SANDRA: On my first day of school I felt a little weird because I didn't understand my teacher or the kids that talked to me. There were a lot of people that talked to me, and I don't really know what it means. So it was a little hard, my first day of school. The days went by and then I started to know words, like hard words, and then I started to talk. The hard days were when they say words I didn't even understand and big words that were hard. There were a lot of people that talked to me the first days and I didn't really understand them.

Mexico, Missouri has 11,320 inhabitants. According to the 2000 census, ninety-nine of them are "Hispanic." Sandra and her family say the real boom in the town's Mexican immigrant population has begun since then. Native-born residents have been heading elsewhere to live, leaving a local factory without anyone to fill the night shifts. Immigrants like them, they said, were willing to take the jobs.

Sandra's mom said the first to arrive were Mexican young men, tired of picking grapes in California. They brought their friends, and some of these friends brought their wives. And in October 2000, Sandra and Charley became the first Mexican kids in Mexico, Missouri.

Sandra was born in La Compañía Jutla, a small town in Mexico's southern Oaxaca state. Though her grandparents lived off the corn and beans they raised on their small property, her parents, Juana and Fernando, had gotten some education and decent work. Juana had studied through junior high, while Fernando had joined the armed forces.

Sandra's parents met and married in the small Oaxacan pueblo, but they soon left home for the city of Saltillo, Coahuila, where Fernando worked at a military base. No sooner was Sandra born than her parents continued their search for opportunity in *la capital*, Mexico City. Sandra's mom worked as a housemaid in the wealthy Coyoacán neighborhood, while her dad joined the city police force.

After their second child, Carlos—now known as Charley—was born, the family of four could not make ends meet. So when Juana's brother decided to cross the border to work in the fields of California, her husband Fernando went with him.

After six months in the fields, picking grapes and tomatoes with thousands of his countrymen, Fernando returned to Mexico. He wanted to continue working in California, but with his wife. His kids would remain in Mexico City for the time being, with relatives.

After contracting a coyote, or smuggler, to help lead them on the dangerous trip across the desert, the couple was caught four times and returned to Mexico. But for Sandra's parents, the fifth time was the charm.

Sandra's mom still shudders when she discusses the trip. Like many of the hundreds of thousands of Mexicans who have crossed the border since the mid-1990's, Juana has no thoughts of returning to Mexico temporarily. She will remain in the United States until she is positive she's ready to return to Mexico for good. "If I return to Mexico," she says, "I won't come back here anymore. The crossing is horrible."

The couple arrived in the farming community of Selma, California and began working in the fields. Soon, they sent for their kids. Not wanting to put the children's lives at risk with a dangerous desert crossing, the couple hired someone to sneak them across with fake papers. Six-year-old Sandra had to impersonate the girl whose documents she carried.

SANDRA: They asked me questions, what was the name of the girl? And I forgot about her name. And that was the big problem. The man told me what was the name and the man that asked me the question said, "No, you be quiet." Then I said the name. They didn't check the bags like they usually do because there were too many people coming. They said, "Well, go, go on." I was kind of scared when they asked me for the name and I didn't even know it. Yeah, I was scared.

No sooner had the children arrived in Selma than the couple met some countrymen who were off to work in Missouri. They were headed to factory jobs, they said, where conditions were far better than in the fields. So they set off for the state of Missouri, to a place called Mexico. Within days the couple was working at a nearby factory alongside other Mexicans and "Mexicoans," as the town's residents call themselves.

As soon as Sandra's dad began work, his supervisors went to the school district to enroll Sandra and Charley. Within days of the family's arrival, a school representative had come to their home to teach them basic words in English so they could get by in the classroom. Before the week was over, the siblings had made Mexico, Missouri history as they entered the school's gates.

Sandra and Charley were not the only ones to feel confused and overwhelmed—their mother remembers it as well. "We felt—I don't know how, because they all spoke only English and we only spoke Spanish," she recalls. "We didn't understand a thing. We've only learned a little bit of English, but it is so hard and nobody, but nobody, spoke Spanish, with the exception of the one lady who did translation."

Sandra's mom says Sandra learned English in five months, but Sandra disagrees. "I think there were four months, or less, like three months," she says. Just a year after arriving in the United States, eight-year-old Sandra carries on full conversations in English, though she often wrinkles her nose tightly and determinedly, throwing her eyes to the ceiling in search of a particular word or phrase.

When she asks her best friend's mom, a Missouri-born Mexicoan, for help in finding one of these words, she does so without reverting to Spanish. In fact, Sandra already seems to prefer speaking in English—so much so that the occasional taunts of classmates roll right off her back.

> SANDRA: When I started to speak a little more English, a boy named Paul started to be mean to me. He said, "You're never going to speak English." Then when I started to speak more English, he stopped talking to me, and my mom went and talked to the teacher and told her he was being too mean to me. So he stopped doing that, and then he just talked to me; he didn't do nothing to me.

The school has made an impressive effort to reach out to Sandra's family. One teacher had her report cards translated into Spanish so Juana could read them, and the school tries to provide a translator for parent-teacher conferences. And when the school cannot give translation, Juana often can bring along her workplace's translator to help her out.

Meanwhile the Mexicans keep coming. Juana already has three brothers and a sister in Mexico, Missouri. "There are a lot of us Mexicans in the factory," she says. "There used to be about 40 of us, but now there are a lot more than that."

Stores like Country Mart and Derby's have begun to stock products for the immigrants. "When we got here," says Juana, "the only Mexican food they had was flour tortillas. We don't like flour tortillas, and it was hard because the kids didn't like to eat them either. Now there are corn tortillas and beans. Now we eat much better."

Just one year after the family arrived, Mexico, Missouri's first Mexican restaurant opened in a strip mall, across the parking lot from McDonald's. Mexicoans practice Spanish there with the waiters, who—along with a growing number of Mexico's Mexicans— have picked up a good deal of English.

Juana has not advanced too far in learning the language of her new country, but her desire for her kids to speak English has come to outweigh all other concerns. "We might want to return to Mexico, but not right now," says Juana. "I would like Sandra to study through junior high here, and then we could return to Mexico. I want Sandra and Charley to learn English."

SANDRA: What's different about school from Mexico is that they here talk in English. I like school better here because I want to learn English. I already know Spanish. I got one hundred percent on the very first spelling test I had. In my second one I didn't because they're a little more hard words. I wanted to keep up with the class so I worked so hard. I thought they were doing fun things and I wanted to keep up with them. I want to be a doctor, or if I can't be a doctor I want to be a teacher. When I grow up I want to live in Mexico, where I'm from. My whole family is there. I want to see my grandma and my grandpa. I miss them.

The mother of Sandra's best friend is on call to answer homework questions, and when Sandra cannot get in touch with her, she takes her questions directly to the teacher. Juana says Sandra has been doing well in school, although she herself cannot help with homework. Usually, things work the other way around—eight-year-old Sandra translates for her mom. Answering the phone is daily duty for Sandra, but sometimes her translating responsibilities extend even to doctor's visits. The work is difficult for a young girl. "Sometimes they are talking too fast!" exclaims Sandra. "I want to say, "Um, can you talk a little more slowly?" But they are still talking; they don't even let me talk. Sometimes I don't want to translate because they talk too fast."

Sandra also translates for newly arrived kids at school. While she may have been the first Mexican in Mexico, Missouri's school system, within the last year dozens of others have joined her. "There's my cousin, who's in my grade," she says, "and then there's Edgar, and Olivia, and Mariana…" The count stops at about fifteen other Mexican kids, who all arrived within the last year.

Asked if she is happy that there are now more Mexican kids at school, Sandra only shrugs her shoulders. "It doesn't make a difference," she says. After all, though she was born in Mexico, her new best friend and two favorite kickball partners were born in Mexico, too. (Missouri)

Rodrigo, the Anthropologist

RODRIGO: When I was on the bus, heading to the border, I imagined that I would be teaching to a classroom of white children.

The bus would end its long journey north in Nuevo Laredo, Tamaulipas, but most of its passengers would continue north. Rodrigo Rubio sat surrounded by the Mexicans who were on their way to staff the kitchens, the fields, and the construction sites of California, Texas, Arizona, Michigan, and Nebraska. To get there, some would swim rivers, others would trek deserts. Rodrigo had heard one or two died every day trying to get across. It was very hot that September in 1999.

Rodrigo would not risk it. He would cross the line with a tourist visa, as his wife and seven children had done two months ago. In his head he saw the future with the wisdom of the Aztec sages whose lives he had studied in the highlands of Mexico. In his bag was a photo of his son Esdra, newly buried in a Mexico City graveyard.

The bus stopped, and Rodrigo joined the mass of Mexicans and Americans, some with, some without a passport, who crossed the bridges into Laredo, Texas. The border official, a dark haired man who could have come from Rodrigo's hometown, hardly looked at him and said "Welcome," signaling the next person in line to advance.

Rodrigo boarded another bus to his final destination, Charlotte, North Carolina. His sister-in-law, who had moved there some time ago, had offered her home to his entire family. Charlotte has the fourth fastest-growing Hispanic population in the United States. Many of the Mexican immigrants Rodrigo knew had gone to North Carolina to fill job shortages in the agricultural sector, or in the sun-belt's booming construction industry, as well as its furniture production and service sectors. But these jobs were not in Rodrigo

Rubio's plans. He thought he would eventually land in a classroom teaching anthropology as he had in Mexico.

RODRIGO: I used to say to my wife that the situation in Mexico allowed us barely to survive, but it just wasn't enough money. So when we decided to come, we thought we were going to make a complete change in the life of our family. I speak Nahuatl, the language of the Aztecs. My research was on Aztec culture. I know how to interpret the Aztec and Maya codices. I was a teacher of social sciences in my country. I arrived here and knew there were opportunities for everyone, but where?

Rodrigo holds a degree from Mexico City's National School of Anthropology, and his personality is far more intellectual than practical. Even when the family's economic situation was in dire straits in Mexico, he kept buying books. "Instead of bringing home this book, why don't you bring us something to eat?" his sensible wife would ask. Rather than stop buying, Rodrigo simply began to hide the books on his way in. When their three-year-old son Esra died of leukemia, they borrowed money for a casket and flowers.

Rodrigo and María conducted a family vote, and all decided to try their luck in the United States. María went first, and soon Rodrigo followed. When he arrived, his wife had begun work in a factory, and his children had enrolled in school; the older ones worked nights. The nine Rubios slept on the floor of one bedroom in the house of María's sister.

"The Anthropologist," as Charlotte's Mexicans know Rodrigo, found a directory of book publishers and carefully wrote letters to each, seeking to publish a diary he had written about his son's suffering. "And all the machines that answered me in English—I didn't even know what they were saying—cut down my greatest desire," he says. "And with a lump in my throat and a lot of worrying, we ran out of money."

Just one month after his arrival, Rodrigo decided enough was enough. He wanted to return to Mexico, "where a person lives freely." His wife did not. A daughter said she would go to Mexico with her father. Two sons said they would stay on with their mother. As he watched his family teeter on the brink of collapse, Rodrigo realized he no longer had a choice. He would have to find a way to make it in North Carolina.

Rodrigo kept reading his anthropology books at night, but began spending his days working in a factory. Then his family received word that housing restrictions made living in Maria's sister's small apartment illegal. She told them they had to leave. Suddenly, the Rubios were homeless.

> RODRIGO: We didn't own anything, not a blanket or a cup or a spoon. We went looking for apartments, and we really had our pockets emptied. They charged $40 for each application. We applied in three places, and you never get that money back. Those $120 could have been enough for us to eat for, say, a month. Instead it was all wasted. Finally my wife visited one place and there was a Mexican woman working there. And she told my wife, "I'll help you." And she did. So we began by eating on the floor, because we did not have anything. We didn't have furniture, nothing. Until one day we were in a furniture shop, and there was a Costa Rican woman who worked there. And she said, I am going to help you buy furniture. See? Here is a chair she helped us buy. She gave my wife credit to buy mattresses to sleep on; she helped us get beds because we were sleeping on the floor. She gave me credit and I got this kitchen table and with my daughter's credit we got this living room furniture and…what happened next? Little by little we have been getting the things we need.

Having credit was a great advantage. Most of Rodrigo's friends spent much of their income cashing paychecks, paying off loans at the pawn shop, and paying extreme fees for money transfers to Mexico (and never really knowing how many pesos were being given for the dollars). Though the interest rates were not as good as the credit union or local bank (later he would discover he could use financial institutions), he was able to acquire the things needed in a home in the U.S. First the family acquired a secondhand couch, then a table. Then, a television and a VCR. After a year they moved into a house—with five bedrooms and three bathrooms. They are the first Latinos on their block. "A little bit at a time," says "the anthropologist" of his family's progress in Charlotte. America is about working "like a robot."

"Don't talk," floor bosses tell the former academic lecturer. "Don't let your mind wander because if you mess up, we'll take it out of your salary. You can have that drink of water after you finish your work. Why are you going to the bathroom when you've already been twice?" Indeed, factory work was not like teaching anthropology.

RODRIGO: I never, ever would have thought, as a teacher, as an anthropologist, with knowledge of world cultures, that I would be working in this kind of place. Often the younger people make fun of me. They call you old, they call you tired; they call you grandpa and don't show you respect. This really gets me down sometimes. I have seen elderly people come out of the factory really injured in their legs, and they don't say anything because otherwise they will tell him he's too old, and what are you doing here anyway? So you see fifteen-year-old children, like my kids, in factories. We got them papers that say they're older so they can work, which are really common around here. The motto of my Hispanic supervisor is, "If you're sick, why would you come to work? You're no use to me. If your head hurts or your hand hurts, why do you come to work?" Well, our motto as workers is, "If I don't work, I don't eat." So even when my wife is sick, she goes to work. Even really sick, she has to go.

The majority of the factory's workers are Mexicans, although some come from other Latin American countries, and some African-Americans work in a different part of the same plant. Two white U.S. Americans came to work there, but they quit within a few days.

Rodrigo: People say Mexicans are very hard working. I don't know. I believe all new people who see the opportunities in this country are willing to work hard to advance. Yes, we are willing to work very hard. We are all over this country, working, working, working. Yes, I guess we are hard working...maybe like the first Americans, maybe like the first pioneers.

Factory work hardly satisfies Rodrigo, but he says he is determined not to become desperate. He invokes a Mexican saying—"Problems, with bread, are good," he says. "As long as we're eating, we have to continue fighting."

As he speaks in Spanish, Rodrigo talks openly of his American dreams. Although his English is still limited, he is becoming an American in the best way he knows how—by reading books. No sooner did he arrive in North Carolina than he began to look for ways to adjust his outlook and values to the environment surrounding him, and to follow the lead of the people he admires.

RODRIGO: When I arrived in the United States, I started to look at important people from here, like Martin Luther King. I studied his life. For Americans, for Asians, for whomever, Martin Luther King is an example. He was pastor of a church. He was part of a race that was marginalized in that time, yet his principal philosophy was based in Mahatma Gandhi. If God gave us this brain, we have to use it for something. I'm trying to fill it with information every day because I like thinking and philosophy.

Rodrigo has rested from the exhausting struggle to publish the book about his son, Esdra's sickness, but in the meantime he hangs the child's photo on the wall of his new house. A brother-in-law came to Charlotte from Mexico and brought with him the family's large coat of arms. To the names of the nine living family members, Rodrigo added along the side, E-S-D-R-A. The house, the furniture, the coat of arms—all are now in Charlotte. In Mexico City sits an apartment, fully paid-off, full of furniture and books but empty of people. He and his wife take turns wanting to stay or go back, but meanwhile they are making progress.

RODRIGO: Now that we've been here for a few years, we can see the results. And one of these results is that my children have learned maybe not perfect English, but wherever they go they can have a conversation with anyone in English. And the other goal we've achieved is to have a house, something that in Mexico you could work your whole life and never achieve. What is the American way? Each person pays his own way, and everyone works. In Mexico, I worked for the entire family. But you get here and you confront a situation where your son tells you, "You know what, Dad? I am working, but I'm not going to give you my salary. It's mine. I am your son, but it's my money." And the son is within his right to say, "I'm not going to give you a cent." Listen, but what about the house! Your mother! "I want my own life already." This was not how we thought in Mexico. Why do things change here? Quiet! "Don't tell me to be quiet. Don't yell at me." Go to your room. "I'm not going." I'll make you go. "I'll report you to the police." Unbelievable!

Even as he faces the challenge of raising children in another culture and feels his hands become arthritic from the factory work, Rodrigo's idealistic side continues to get the best of him. "He continues insisting," his wife says. "He doesn't know how long it will take, but he wants to work as the teacher he is."

English has not come naturally, and Rodrigo has found neither time nor money to take classes. But he and his friends are starting an organization to serve Charlotte's exploding Mexican population, and Rodrigo Rubio has plans.

RODRIGO: Tomorrow our group is going to start looking for an English teacher. We have so many programs we want to start, and sometimes we have to spend money from our own pockets even though we have so little. But it will happen, one day. Maybe I will start teaching anthropology to the children of Mexican families so they won't forget their heritage. Maybe I was never meant to teach whites about the Aztecs. Maybe I am supposed to teach Mexican Americans about Mexico!

Lucía, the Grape Picker

Lucía's three years in central California have turned her world upside-down, but somehow, in suspension she keeps moving forward. First, the people she trusted most betrayed her; then on September 11, 2001, as for so many Americans, her life became filled with a terror from which she has yet to escape.

Lucía is twenty-six years old. She arrived in 1998 to the farming community of Earlimart, California from Mazatlán, Sinaloa. For over a hundred years, Mexicans have left their homes to pick grapes and strawberries in California. The multi-billion dollar agricultural economy of California depends on them. Many of Lucía's coworkers in the fields are members of Mexico's newest group of migrants, the indigenous people of southern states like Oaxaca. Migrants with more education and basic skills have started to avoid the brutal conditions of farm work in California's Central Valley.

Having completed a year of university-level psychology training, Lucía is an exception to this rule. Today, her schooling is limited to the *escuelita* ("little school") she attends at 6:30 a.m. each morning, before beginning her day in the grape fields. In this *escuelita* she learns about grapes—when to pick them, when not to. The knowledge proves useless, however, when field bosses insist their workers pick even unripened grapes, hiding them beneath beautiful ripe ones in the packaging.

Her boyfriend, Ricardo, also works with grapes—he prunes, she packages. But the work is not year-round, and when their first grape season came to an end, they sought assistance from an aunt in San Pedro, just south of Los Angeles. For new arrivals relatives from Mexico tended to be the first line of defense versus social workers, employment agencies, and free housing. But not in her case, says Lucía, gesturing intently with perfectly-painted nails. The couple arrived with their suitcases, but the aunt's home was not open to them. The aunt said she was afraid the two would track bugs into her house along with their bags.

LUCÍA: She is a citizen; she became a citizen here. She doesn't have kids. And I told her, "Auntie," I called her on the phone, "Help me because you are a citizen, you don't have kids, you could register me, I am your family. All other families help each other. That is supposed to be the Mexican way. I would help you if you were not a citizen." And she told me, "I'll see, I don't know," and she never did anything. She could have submitted papers for me, or legally adopted me, or something. She is a citizen, she has been here for many years, and I don't know how but I know she could have helped me. But no. She has no children, she could never have kids, and she could have helped me. But no.

The aunt said Lucía and Ricardo would have to "scratch with their own nails." While the two looked for work in Los Angeles, they slept in a used car junkyard. "I was there in the car yard, thinking, it would have been better just to have stayed where the grapes are – even if all we eat is instant soup," says Lucía.

Rejected by her aunt, Lucía sought help from cousins. Once again, she was turned away.

LUCÍA: I feel alone. I only have Ricardo. I shouldn't feel alone because I have him, and he has me. But sometimes I want to see my family, to visit them, no? But they look at you like an alien, as though you smell bad or have an incurable disease. They look at you strangely. Since they have been here for so many years, my cousins already speak good English, and they have good jobs. I asked them help me find a job, even if it's sweeping the floor or something. But they didn't help me at all.

Stunned, the couple returned to the fields, where they earn $6.25 per hour. In the farming community of Earlimart, where at least ninety percent of the 6,583 inhabitants are "Hispanic,"[2] they settled into a trailer they rented from a woman they knew from Mexico. She charged them $200 weekly for room and board, well above the housing's value in rural California. The trailer had worms and scorpions in the bathroom, Lucía said, and she had to throw salt around to kill them. "It's such an injustice," says Lucía. "We are from the same *rancho*, the same state and everything. How could she have treated us like that when we had just arrived?"

After moving to a second, equally disgusting trailer, the couple finally began to rent a little one-bedroom house. The house is spotless. The floors are painted to look like wood, and satin curtains with red roses cover the windows. The home is fitting for Lucía, whose dyed-blond hair and carefully applied makeup mask the fatigue she says she feels after two years of inhaling pesticides among the grapevines.

The work is hard and thankless, and the pay low. "But I would be content at my job and everything if they didn't act so arrogant, if they didn't abuse people," she says. Her boss, a naturalized Mexican immigrant, regularly yells at her in front of the other workers.

LUCÍA: I stay serious, and I don't like to be chatty with the people I work with. I just expect them to respect me and me them. They don't like it that I don't gossip with them, that I don't make small talk or conversation, but I say it's better this way. So everyone heard when the boss criticized me, and all of them just looked serious, and I kept myself serious. Serious, serious, and I didn't say anything to him. By the afternoon he had calmed down, but everyone had heard the awful things he was saying. He is so cruel and self-important, like, what he cannot do in his house or in other places he takes out on us. People tried to formally complain, but he said, "Fine, sue me. I'll sue you back." Words shouldn't hurt me, but sometimes they do. They hurt because, well, this guy comes from Mexico, the same place we come from. He shouldn't be like that, humiliating people, treating them like trash. He makes us feel like trash, that's how he makes us feel. And everyone is scared to say something, because everyone says what about the job, the job.

Lucía is hoping for an amnesty, so that she can more freely voice her concerns about her workplace. Meanwhile, she feels she cannot complain for fear of deportation, and the conditions at her job remain horrible, she says. At times, the chemical dust on the crops can be so strong she has to stop herself from vomiting.

Lucía dreams of the day she will return to Mexico. There, she says, she and Ricardo will be married and will start a small business together. Lucía wants to plant *chiles* on the small piece of land her grandmother left her, to give work to the unemployed of her *rancho*, "the people who are doing worse than the ones here, without money, with nothing."

But that return is most likely a long way away for this couple. Lucía says she wants to stay at least eight more years, and Ricardo says he simply will not return to Mexico unless he has a green card in hand that will allow him to come back to California without crossing the border illegally. Working for poverty wages in an industry with little room for advancement, speaking Spanish in a community that is almost entirely Mexican, and dreaming of the day they will return to Mazatlán, Lucía and Ricardo seem prime candidates to be "different" immigrants, people who do not want to become U.S. Americans at all. Yet, nothing could be farther from the truth for these two undocumented laborers. They are satisfied to now rent a house, but they dream of buying one. They have already saved money to purchase a pickup truck. "I believe this is the country of opportunity," says Lucía. "The only people who don't progress here are the ones that don't want to."

And that was before September 11. Interviewed just a few weeks after the terrorist attacks on New York, a city farther away from Earlimart than Mazatlán is, Lucía reveals the tremendous transformation that has taken place in her first three years in the United States.

LUCÍA: I have seen these things in the news, when they happen in Colombia and everything, and it does affect me, but this time in New York I felt so pained, so much pain. It pained me so much because innocent people that were going to work, these poor people who had just arrived at their desks, that nothing was going to happen to them and all of a sudden this happens. I spent all day listening to the radio. There I was at work, wondering how could this be. I tell you, the first three days afterwards I couldn't sleep, just thinking, thinking. Seeing the people throwing themselves out the window, just throwing themselves out! We have been to Los Angeles and when I see a building there that's not so big I say, "Look, it seems huge!" Now for someone to throw themselves out, wanting to kill themselves for not wanting to be burned, is something so horrible. Because there were also a lot of Latino people—there were all kinds of people. From here on we are always going to live with a fear that if we go to Los Angeles, who knows what might happen because there was also terror destined for Los Angeles. Since this happened I have felt so traumatized. Those people went to work, and their family members never heard anything more of them. I cried and I cried, and I am just asking God that these people, even if it's just their bodies, appear. Because they are not appearing. After September 11, I somehow feel more American, like this terrible deed was done to me, too. We are all now more American.

Days after millions of Americans awoke to a nightmare, Lucía realized that for her, dreaming the American dream would mean more than saving up to buy a house. It would mean feeling the pain of the American nightmare, too. It would mean that, at least for now, suffering in New York would loom as large for her as—and on some days, larger than—suffering in Mazatlán, Sinaloa.

Miguel, the Iowan

With close-cropped hair, wide-open eyes and a Midwestern accent, Miguel's son, Jorge, looks like a young Iowan boy in a Norman Rockwell painting, just with darker skin. Miguel himself looks distinctly less Norman Rockwell-ish, but the scenes of his life resemble the Americana paintings quite closely.

For this family, the sign that their first four years in the USA have been a success sits on a quiet street in this town of 6,000—their house while Jorge, two of his sisters, and his mother are undocumented, while his two-year-old sister was born a U.S. citizen. Most importantly, his father Miguel is a legal resident. As such, he has been able to secure a "bank loan" at a local credit union. The value of savings, the closeness of family, the ability to open his home to neighbors in need, both Mexican and American—these are the foundations on which Miguel has constructed his family's home.

Miguel is not a recent migrant in the United States, but he is a recent immigrant. He spent the 1970's and 80's going back and forth between Mexico and California. Name a fruit, vegetable, or nut, and Miguel picked it, pruned it, or packaged it during his years as a migrant worker. He spent part of each year in Mexico, and the other part in California, undocumented until he qualified for the amnesty granted to undocumented immigrants in 1986. "Look," says Miguel, "people want to go where they will have the best life. Of the little we earn, we send some back to our families, that's what we do."

In 1993, Miguel was one of the thousands of Mexicans who decided that non-traditional immigration areas held more promise for him than did California. "I realized that in Oklahoma and Iowa there was a lot of work," he says. He decided to try his luck in Omaha, Nebraska.

From Omaha, he began commuting to nearby Red Oak, Iowa, to fill a labor shortage pruning mums in a greenhouse. Soon after, he decided to take up residence there and bring his family.

Because he was in the process of visa renewal, Miguel remained in the United States while his family— at that time, Jorge was two, Pilar was ten, and Teresa was twelve—crossed the border through the harsh desert.

> MIGUEL: Six years ago, when I had just started working here, there weren't other Mexicans. But now there are about thirty of us. Since we're used to working so hard in Mexico, harder than people work here, the work they give you seems easy. This is done, and this, and this, all done! And where will they send us next? The work is fine, a little tiring, but it's work. The one thing is that sometimes you want to look for something else, but you feel timid and scared. You never really look for other jobs, so you never find work that's better, calmer, more enjoyable. We take off the buds. And a week later, the flowers start to open. This past week they sent us to a field where there were 7,300 plants, all good for sale. Just me and four other people. In six days we had done 7,000 something plants. They have like fifteen branches each and you have to take off all the buds from all around. Just any-body without training can't do it well, because you have to be careful to not to knock off the main bulb. The plants we prune are the plants you've seen in stores like Wal-Mart and K-mart.

After six years in the greenhouse, Miguel earns $7 per hour. But careful planning has enabled him to purchase a house in Red Oak, Iowa. A bilingual American friend, Jessica, helped walk them through the process.

Savings and house payments, he says, are his first priority.

> MIGUEL: Jessica, my American friend, says she admires that with the $250 that we each earn in a week, we are paying on a house. The thing is that we don't spend any money eating in restau-rants, or we wouldn't be able to make it on the money we earn. And sometimes, they give us a little overtime and we earn a little

more, right? We don't give allowances to our kids, but once in a while if one of them wants to buy some candy, or some cookies, we'll give to them. But most of the food is here in the house. So we are able to pay off the house. If we went to restaurants like other people we would never have enough money, but this way we do. Sometimes if we get a bonus I go to the bank and we can even get a little ahead on the payments. So we won't always have the house payments hanging over our heads. We're not living large, just making ends meet, more or less. Well, we live like poor people, but we always have clothes, and we're doing better all the time. It's a sacrifice we make, saving our money little by little.

Miguel and Dolores were the first of Red Oak's few hundred Mexican immigrants to own their own home. They are the only Mexicans in their neighborhood—the rest live in another part of the small town.

MIGUEL: We get along really well with the neighbors across the street. They are really old, let's say seventy, and they almost never go out. They just peek out the windows, right? So sometimes if I see a pretty plant, I tell the kids to bring it to her. The neighbor is not just happy, she's delighted. Sometimes when we make tamales, we bring her four or five tamales. She calls us while she's eating them and says, "They're so tasty, and freshly made!" Then, they have a pickup truck, and if we have to throw away something big, they say, "Just tell me and we'll get rid of it for you." Yeah, we've got really nice neighbors here. You have to take care with these things, that's what I say. You have to take care. What I want is to get along well with the neighbors, to go out in the morning and say, "Good morning."

Overall community relations are a bit more strained in this small town than they are for Sandra and her family in Mexico, Missouri. There are some—at least a few—racists in Red Oak, says Miguel. Some people at work do not like to speak to him and his wife. But Miguel is more focused on meeting his loan payments than he is on his responding to them.

MIGUEL: We don't place much importance on it. I mean, they don't offend us. You can see that they don't really like to talk with you, but what can you do? We've got to keep moving forward. We just don't pay much attention to them. It's better that way. But that type of person, you can find them anywhere. I tell my wife, as long as they don't do anything bad to us, we shouldn't do anything bad to anyone else. They go their way, we go ours.

Handling prejudice has been more difficult, however, in the case of their daughter's friends. Some local parents do not want their kids hanging out with Mexicans, and Miguel's kids end up suffering. One friend stopped coming over because of her parents' wishes. Another friend sometimes arrives in tears, hurt by the negative things her mom has said about her Mexican friends.

MIGUEL: Look, our daughters don't smoke, don't drink, nothing. Once, the parents of our daughter's friend stopped letting her come over here because they thought our daughters smoked and drank. One girl's father, though, he finally saw it with his own eyes. Another friend of theirs knew that this father thought poorly of our daughters, and this friend told the father, "They're not the ones who smoke and drink, it's your daughter that smokes and drinks!" She took the father to see it with his own eyes, and the next time he saw our girls he said he was so sorry he had doubted them.

To those who respect him and his family, to both immigrants and American Iowans in need, Miguel has opened his home...and his pocketbook. When new arrivals come from Mexico, the family's home usually becomes their first stop. "They live here while they find an apartment, sometimes for two or three months," says Miguel. But the hospitality is not limited to Mexicans—more than one neighbor has sought refuge from domestic disputes in his house, sometimes with the children.

Miguel also lends money to neighbors, both Mexican and American. "If someone needs $200 or $300, well, of course, my friend," he says quietly.

The five undocumented members of the family— including son Jorge, whose only accent in English is Iowan—are in the process of applying for residency. With Miguel already a resident, they may have a good chance. But regardless of the outcome, the family has begun to make a life for itself in the small town of Red Oak, in the state of Iowa.

1   Thomas Kessner. *The Golden Door: Italian and Jewish Immigrant Mobility in New York City 1880-1815* (New York: Oxford University Press, 1977).

2   U.S. Census 2000.

Part 2:

Down to Business

VIPs On Both Sides of the Border

I visited Chicago many times while working for President Fox. The immigrant community has grown greatly in this Midwestern metropolis. There are many from Guanajuato, from Michoacán, and from far away states like Chiapas. It is one of the cities that has numerous hometown associations and a variety of very verbal political leaders. There are activist leaders who have written books on why Mexicans abroad should be allowed to vote in the Mexican elections. There are militant democrats, republicans, perredistas, panistas and priistas. The Mexican consulate has been one of the most innovative. It conducts programs to provide auto permits for paisanos and tourists, sells health insurance for family members in Mexico, and sponsors many other practical services.

I remember on one of my trips, braceros and family members took over a school cafeteria, demanding that I meet with them and then present to the Mexican government their demands for the return of funds taken during the U.S. bracero program. I believe they were surprised when I did show up (against everyone's advice) and applauded after I listened for over an hour and told them they were VIPs both in Mexico and the U.S. While I could only note and report their grievance back in Mexico City, the fact that I took the time to hear them out and recognize the sincerity of their concern seemed to be meaningful to them.

This is the setting for many like Paola, the informal entrepreneur.

As American As...Owning a Business!

Paola, an undocumented single mother in Atlanta, is perhaps the most "typical" case with her Mexican food business beginning in the informal economy.

What could be more "American" than the immigrant small business owner? Yet, I have come to realize that the phenomenon is more complicated than popular images might make it seem. Is the immigrant narrative of the small business owner supposed to have the immigrant founding an "ethnic" business, or a more "mainstream" one? Is the immigrant supposed to pass the business on to his or her children, or do the kids go on to careers in the professions? Is the dream to make it big thanks to your education, or in spite of the fact that you lack one? And when business owners employ members of their own ethnic group, are they more or less likely to treat those workers with dignity?

Certainly, the small business has solved a number of dilemmas for immigrants who decided to try their luck. It has allowed them to overcome discrimination and language barriers that keep them from advancing in other workplaces, to cash in on their willingness to work ceaselessly, and to be their own bosses.

Mexicans are said to differ from other immigrant groups in that they see their businesses as an end rather than a means. They want their children to inherit their businesses, while Korean or Jewish immigrants preferred for their children to join the professions, most would say.[1]

Thus, according to at least one version of the American immigrant narrative, Mexican immigrants are perhaps the quintessential small business community. Yet, the other side of this story is that Mexican immigrant small businesses have served to strengthen immigrants' ties to Mexico.

This is not just the Mexican immigrant story. This is the story of countless other immigrants from many countries around the world.

Paola, the Informal Entrepreneur

Because she drives her truck around Atlanta each evening selling Mexican food to immigrants, Paola is a good demographer of the city's growing Hispanic population. It was about two years ago, she says, that business started to boom as the Mexican population exploded. And the more immigrants there were, the more immigrants came looking for a taste of home in Paola's cooking. She says that though crossing the border has been harder since September 11, Mexicans keep arriving. "The only time sales go down is in December," she says, when many return to spend Christmas with their families in Mexico.

Born in Zacatelco, Tlaxcala, Paola has always favored going it on her own. Her father was a shoe shiner and her mother a dressmaker, and Paola stopped school at age eleven to help her parents support the family. At age fifteen, she moved out of her parents' house to escape her father's abusive behavior. Living with her godparents, she was the only one of her siblings to leave. She began to work at a thread factory in her hometown, and it was there she met her husband.

The two married and had three children, and Paola soon fell into the role of family breadwinner. She would work in the factory by day, and sell tamales and corn by night. Her husband was usually unemployed. "Funny, huh?" she smiles as she discusses her husband's joblessness. "But it's true."

Paola decided she had to do something to improve her family's situation. Feeling she could not count on her husband to support the family, she called her sister in Atlanta. "I'm coming," she said. Alone. Paola left her kids, then age five, eight, and ten, in her husband's care. "My idea," she says, "was to work really hard," for just eight months before rejoining her family in Zacatelco.

PAOLA: It took a day and half to get to the border, from Zacatelco to Matamoros. From there, you go to a hotel, and call the person.

He knows I'm going to be there. They pick me up and take me to join the group. From there, we walk to the river, like four or five hours. We had to take off our clothes and cross the river. On the other side, there's a car waiting for us. There we have to wait for the Border Patrol to look away. And then we crossed.

Never before, she says, had she left the municipality boundaries of Zacatelco—not even to go to Mexico City, just two hours away.

When she first arrived in Atlanta, Paola moved in with her sister and started to clean houses. Her sister's house was full to capacity, so Paola slept in the closet. "Just the usual for us Hispanics," she says.

To make extra money in the evenings, Paola began to sell corn on the cob, with cheese or mayonnaise on top. The apartment complex where she lived with her sister was largely Hispanic, and she would often make $100 in a single afternoon. The corn sales increased her income significantly, and her stay in Atlanta kept being extended. Eventually, hearing the sound of her children's tears through the telephone became too much. She wanted her kids to join her in Atlanta. She was less sure, however, that she wanted her husband to come.

PAOLA: I wanted to leave my husband there. He asked me to give him another chance, that we would come here together and our lives would change. So I told him it was okay, that I would bring him so that everything would change. But he got here and things didn't get better. He did work, but he never changed. He didn't do anything for us. He didn't care if we had enough to eat, or not. So I told him I couldn't keep living this way.

Soon after his arrival, Paola and her husband divorced. "You come here," she says, "and the woman starts to have other ideas. We don't have to put up with husbands like him any more." To provide for her children, she began to sell her food to more and more customers. Soon, her work as a maid became too much. Working with another woman, Paola would have to clean four homes in a day, often leaving no time even to eat. It was simply too exhausting. Housecleaning, she says, "is really difficult work—sticking your hands in the toilets of the Americans," she says with a laugh. Although she earned $300 a week in addition to the food sales money she earned at night, she quit after several months to focus on her food sales.

At one point, she also tried working in a cardboard factory by day, while continuing her food business at night. But the demand for food was greater all the time. "People wanted my Mexican food," she says. "Tamales, mole, tostadas, tacos, chile rellenos." Factory work made it difficult to pick the kids up from school, and if they were sick she couldn't get permission to stay home with them. For Paola, it wasn't worth it. In the end, she decided that self-employment with her winning recipes was the way to go.

Her sales continued to grow, and soon she decided to make an investment. In 2001, she bought a truck equipped as a mobile restaurant. She spent her days cooking at home, and from five until nine at night drove around Atlanta delivering food to established customers and knocking on doors to find new ones. She now sells 200-250 tamales each week, a large proportion to patrons from her hometown of Zacatelco. Her daughters, ages eleven and fourteen, accompany her on delivery runs. Her business sells $250-$300 in one day, she says, but that is not pure profit. "You've got to take some of that money to invest back in the business," she says. "You have to invest."

Paola's reason for preferring to run her own business rather than being someone's employee sounds similar to most entrepreneurs.

> PAOLA: I earn more, and I'm my own boss. It's much better because I am with my daughters. If they get sick, I don't need to ask anybody's permission to spend a day at home with them. When I go out to sell, I don't have to leave them alone. We share the work between us, and that feels really good.

Paola says at some point in the future she would like to open a restaurant—the kind without wheels. When she first arrived in Atlanta eight years ago, there were fewer Mexican restaurants, but today there are many. "I think Americans like Mexican food a lot, too." But she knows she will have to wait until she has legalized her status. Being undocumented, she says, poses a lot of obstacles to running a more official small business. Even now it is a problem; although she drives around each night to earn a living, she does not have a driver's license and thus cannot buy insurance. Once, this even landed her in jail.

PAOLA: I was out driving with my kids, and the police stopped me. They didn't say I was doing anything wrong, like speeding or anything. I think they just suspected I was driving without a license! So I called my sister, and she came for my kids, and then they took me to jail. I had to call friends and relatives and ask them to loan me money so I could pay the fine to get out of jail, which was about $1,200. For us here in Atlanta, the penalty for driving without a license is something we have to think about— what if this happens? Because they stop you a lot just because you look Hispanic.

Sometimes, says Paola, life as an undocumented immigrant in Atlanta makes it easy to be nostalgic for Mexico—for the agricultural life and the open spaces. But her small, informal business is growing each day, and she thinks she owes it to her kids to stay where they will have opportunities. "It's either go back to Mexico and eat from the land," she says, "or stay here and get educated."

1   Ibid.

President Vicente Fox and Hernandez.

Marzo 21, 1996

Juan:

Nunca tendremos forma de agradecerte a nombre de todos los Guanajuatenses lo que has hecho por tu tierra en estos dias! Especialmente por los pobres, por los desempleados, por los emmigrantes, por los Jovenes.
Con personajes como tu, no hay duda, Guanajuato será "TIERRA DE oportunidades" Muchas Gracias! DURO!

President Fox Letter to Hernandez.

Carlos Flores, Hernandez and Juan Antonio Fernandez — first fulltimers on
Fox campaign.

President Jimmy Carter and Hernandez.

Hernandez and Mikael Gorbachev.

Hernandez and Mohammed Ali.

Juan Jr., Texas Governor Rick Perry and Hernandez.

Novelist Mario Vargas Llosa and Hernandez.

Novelist Carlos Fuentes and Hernandez.

Rob Allyn and Hernandez.

Hernandez and Dick Morris.

Hernandez and Senator John McCain.

President Bush, Hernandez and President Fox.

Part 3:

God Across the Border

Is God a Mexican?

While I cannot easily categorize or even explain the intensely personal role that religion has played in the lives of migrants, what I can say with certainty is that religious institutions, both for their spiritual and their communal content, have been the central axis of daily life for hundreds of immigrants I have met. I also believe this is true for millions of others in the history of the United States. In a society of religious pluralism, immigrants have congregated in existing religious institutions and established new ones of their own.

Some, like Mexican migrant Rigoberto profiled in this chapter, considered themselves to be very religious in their countries of origin and sought out a religious life from the moment they arrived in the new land. Others gravitated to the church as an axis of stability in the constantly-rotating world of the new immigrant.

I know some people think that separate Spanish and English masses or services constitute a negative "separatism" on the part of Mexican immigrants, but this chapter shows that religious institutions have utilized these Spanish-language portals to integrate new immigrants into their larger religious communities. Furthermore, I believe the separation of immigrants in their religious institutions is not a fact, but rather, a tension in the history of immigrant religion.

So many of the religious institutions that form the landscape of America were founded by newcomers. German and British immigrants founded the Methodist Church, and Irish and Italians founded the Catholic churches of the United States. In some cases, most notably the Catholic church, successive immigrant generations have been seated in the same pews as the children and grandchildren of previous immigrant groups. In other cases, groups like Koreans and African-Americans have formed their own churches, creating separate communities where integration into existing ones was undesirable or impossible.

The personal stories profiled in this chapter show that both ways have their followers among Mexican immigrants. While large cities have tended to foster separate immigrant religious communities, in the "new" Mexican immigrants in the South and the Midwest I have encountered clergy more determined to keep their congregations together.

Mexicans in the United States are also less religiously homogenous than some might think. Back in Mexico, the 2000 Census showed that twelve percent did not identify themselves as Catholic. The states of Mexico's newer migrations from the South are also the ones with higher Protestant populations, such as Chiapas, where twenty-two percent of the population says it is Protestant[1] (though Protestant churches themselves estimate much more).

One such Chiapaneco immigrant, Rigoberto, is one of less than a dozen Mexicans attending Owensboro Protestant Church of Owensboro, Kentucky. As Owensboro's small Mexican immigrant community grows, its clergy say they are determined not to go the way of the "Spanish mass" and "English mass," but rather, to keep their religious services bilingual and their communities integrated.

Though Mexico's Jewish community numbers just 50,000,[2] it has contributed several thousand emigrants to the United States, and I have met some of them in my travels. Zejaria "Zeji" Ozeri and San Diego's Mexican Jews tend to be bilingual and work in "mainstream" work environments. Still, many prefer to maintain institutions separate from the established Jewish community in order to ensure that their children speak Spanish and maintain their ties to Mexican culture.

In all of these scenarios, clergy have become the front-line of immigrant assistance, acting as pastors, social workers, English teachers, psychologists and even immigration lawyers. It is clergy who fill the gaps left by local and federal governments, particularly for undocumented immigrants. A case in point is Patricia, whose American-born priest has supported her through her arrival to a new country and the death of her father.

And, though I focus on those who have made religion a large part of their lives, it is important to note that many Mexicans in the United States choose not to affiliate themselves with any particular religion or institution.

Rigoberto, the First Mexican in Church

Rigoberto might not agree that in matters congregational, Mexican immigrants must stick together. The only thing Rigoberto has in common with the people he calls "family" is faith. From a small town on Mexico's southern border with Guatemala, he barely gets by in English, the language of his co-parishioners and of his church service. But Owensboro Protestant Church of Owensboro, Kentucky, the soft-spoken Mexican immigrant says, is the closest thing to a family he has.

One of nine siblings, Rigoberto is the son of farmers. His birth town of Comalapa, in Chiapas, one of Mexico's poorest states, could offer him few opportunities. So at the age of fifteen, he moved to the state capital of Tuxtla Gutierrez to study accounting. Working his way through school, he soon was supporting his mother, who followed him to Tuxtla.

Work and study were important, but church was always most important.

RIGOBERTO: Yes, since I was young I had this privilege of being able to be a part of, to congregate with, to attend, and slowly but surely to grow closer in the church. I was introduced to this when I was young, and I feel it's really important. It is the most basic thing that should exist in a person—recognizing that God exists. Because what would we be without God in our hearts? It would be an unpleasant and unordered life.

Rigoberto has tried to live a life of order and faith from the start. In Tuxtla Gutiérrez, he started working for a company that bred flies for agricultural uses. He stayed with the same company for fifteen years, advancing professionally while supporting his mother and siblings.

When his mother died several years ago, he went into a depression. He quit his job and searched for a calling to lift him from his sadness. He needed to try something new. After a brief time as a snack salesman, Rigoberto realized he would not be able to make ends meet. In the year 2000, he followed a friend's tip and crossed the border illegally to go work in Owensboro, Kentucky. "And now," he says, "here I am."

Rigoberto migrated for personal reasons even more than for financial ones. While many immigrants have unrealistically high expectations of life in the United States, Rigoberto, who focused more on the moral aspects of migration, expected the worst.

> RIGOBERTO: Here, people suffer, too. You don't think straight or feel centered. Sometimes I don't even know what to do, and maybe I could fall into alcoholism or drugs. But it's important to have your head on straight and to be strong in order to make it, because it's difficult to be so far from your family. It could possibly reach the point of falling into desperation and vice. There are some young people who say, "I've got money, I'm going to go have fun and maybe get drunk." But that's not happiness, that's not right. There are always people that fall into those kinds of vices all over the world. But there are also people who come here to improve themselves. This makes me happy, that they improve themselves. That's why I came here, because of the desire to improve myself.

In Daviess County, where Owensboro is the largest city, U.S. Census data put the number of Hispanics at 845 in the year 2000—about one percent of the population. The actual numbers are probably much higher, says Rigoberto. Mexican immigrants first came to Owensboro to pick tobacco. About three quarters of Kentucky's tobacco farmers are Mexican,[3] and Rigoberto says the immigrants, many from his hometown of Comalapa, soon branched into the service industry as well. Rigoberto's first stop was a chicken plant, and later, he became the maintenance man in a warehouse.

Since he arrived in Owensboro, Rigoberto—who has never been married—moved into a small, two-bedroom house with four other immigrants from Chiapas. But even Owensboro's growing Mexican immigrant population does not give Rigoberto the same sense of home and family that his church does.

RIGOBERTO: In Mexico, in the United States, or in any part of the world you go, it's important to find the church of Christ, the people of God. I feel great here because I really appreciate my brothers in the church. I didn't know anyone here, but it is always the duty of every Christian to find the church. We need to have this communion. We are a people, we are a body, and that's the interesting part. So after I arrived, I looked in the phone book under "Protestant churches," and I called them.

Rigoberto's first day at Owensboro Protestant was also Owensboro Protestant's first day with a Mexican immigrant. No Spanish was spoken. Nonetheless, he says, from the first moment he has felt more at home at Owensboro Protestant than he would at a party with other Mexicans. Fitting in has been a preoccupation of his, and he knows English is the key to doing so. "With the help of God," he says, "I want to learn some English so I can get along with the American people. I feel like it's necessary."

Indeed, the only thing on the walls of his simply-decorated duplex are papers from English lessons. "Clapped," says one. "Walked," says another.

Learning and evangelizing, too, are key aspects of faith for Rigoberto.

RIGOBERTO: It's important to invite people to accept Jesus Christ. And if they are controlled by vices, I want to invite them to leave those vices. Here in the United States they say everyone is Christian. But it's very easy to say that—living it is another matter. It's important to teach, like in any other type of studies. If I'm studying Spanish, math or English, I have to start at the beginning. So in this case, we teach them the truth of God's plan for mankind, to read the Bible. We tell them, "This is the word of God, which we read and obey, which we live." So it's important to teach them from the simplest to the most, the most— maybe things they couldn't understand, I couldn't understand. I myself need to learn more, I need to know more. We need to know more to not remain stagnant, to keep moving forward.

A year after Rigoberto arrived at Owensboro Protestant, there were about a half-dozen Mexicans attending prayer services, and one Spanish-speaking Sunday School teacher, Rigoberto. For their benefit, the pastor greets congregants in Spanish every Sunday, and invites Mexicans to lead other parts of the service in Spanish as well. Rigoberto likes the mix. He hopes eventually he will be able to start giving entire sermons in Spanish, just as he did back in Mexico.

Will the Spanish-speaking population of Owensboro Protestant continue to grow? Owensboro, in many ways, exemplifies the openness towards Mexican immigrants that many small towns in America's heartland have displayed. Church members volunteer to give Rigoberto private English classes. Community college Spanish lessons fill up with Kentuckians anxious to communicate with their new neighbors. Some farmers even travel to Mexico to meet their workers' families. "I appreciate that when we go shopping, they treat us well," says Rigoberto. "Maybe a smile, a goodbye. The city is friendly and respectful, and I feel like I'm in my own hometown."

Rigoberto has not been back to Mexico since he arrived in Kentucky. He does not want to cross illegally again, but believes that God will intervene to assure him legal status. His pastor has already attempted to file the papers, but missed a deadline because they were sent to a wrong address. Nonetheless, Rigoberto's story appeared, with full name and photo, in the local newspaper. No one in Owensboro blinked an eye about it. Nobody was surprised to learn that most of the immigrants the Owensboro economy depends on are in Kentucky without legal papers. "God will see to it that things work out," Rigoberto says. "I am not afraid."

Patricia, the Church Women's Leader

For Patricia, church has been an antidote to fear. After the trauma of crossing the border illegally, the support of her Staten Island priest has been indispensable to her emotional survival.

PATRICIA: When I crossed over with the three kids the first time, it was really difficult and dangerous. We almost died. The border patrol caught us and detained us for twelve hours. They didn't treat us badly or anything, but I felt terrified, because this was just not for me. Everyone else was calm because this had happened to them before, but I didn't sleep. I stayed up all night wondering what would happen if someone came in and took one of my kids. I was terrified. In the morning they sent us back to Nogales.

The second time we went in a van. But they started to drive faster and faster, and the brakes failed. There were thirty of us in one van, and we were being burned by the heat coming up from the floor of the van. The children started to scream, and the guy stopped the van and told us, "Get out, get out, because the van's going to explode!'" So we ran.

The crossing was much worse than Patricia could ever have imagined when she begged her husband, Antonio, to let her come join him in Staten Island. Antonio had been in the United States, off and on, for five years before she arrived. The loneliness back in Mexico was nearly unbearable for Patricia, but there seemed to be no other choice. The family earned just $3 a day there, and the couple's lifestyle got worse, not better, with each passing year. "Every time the kids advanced one level in school, our economic situation went down one level," she recalls. Patricia supplemented the income she received from her husband's remittances with pesos she earned here and there selling shoes and clothing. Even then, the economic struggle, combined with the pain of loneliness, started to drive Patricia to desperation.

PATRICIA: I spoke with my husband, and I said, "I don't know what to do, because it isn't enough money." He said, "No, but if you come here, we will be even less able to make ends meet. If we can't do it with you changing the dollars into pesos, here we'll die of hunger." And I just begged him over and over. I said, "Please, I want to go there with you. I can't be here for another year." I felt very alone more than anything else. So we decided that I would come. I told him, "You're not going to regret this. If I say I'm going to the United States, I will have to make things work." And thank God, we're not rich, but our situation is good.

On arrival to Staten Island, Patricia was determined to contribute economically to the family's well being, as she had promised her husband she would. She started working as a babysitter's assistant for $20 per day. Like Rigoberto in Owensboro, Patricia looked for a church—a Catholic church—shortly after she arrived. There, they found a bilingual priest anxious to support them emotionally, and to help them support themselves economically.

PATRICIA: After I arrived in this country, about two months later I approached the church. I went to the Father's office and intro-duced myself to him. I asked if he would please help me find work. He said, "Well, what do you know how to do?" And I said, "Father, in Mexico I didn't work, I was just in the house with my five kids, taking care of them." And he said, "What do you think you can do?" I said, "Well, I think here the one thing I could do would be to clean houses." He said, "Okay, if you want to work, I will have you clean the church." I felt like it was a great test for me. It was like a blessing from God to be in the parish with the father.

"Great job," the father told Patricia. She continued to clean for the church. Six months later the father said, "I have heard of some priests in the Bronx who help women with no jobs. I would like you to help me do something like that."

Patricia accompanied the priest to some meetings in the Bronx to observe the unemployed women's groups. Within the month, Patricia had begun a similar committee at her Staten Island church. The group taught women tricks of the house-cleaning trade, and helped them figure out how much to charge their clients. Patricia was named as the committee president, and within the year, the trainings had turned from furniture dusting to leadership building. At the end of the year, about thirty women counted themselves members of the committee.

PATRICIA: The father asked me if I knew how to cook Mexican dishes. He said, "If you want to sell at the church, you have permission. If you don't have a job, why don't you sell something at the church?" I decided to make tamales. Now, a man named Ramón who has been going to the church for twenty years, calls me "The Tamale Queen." Always green tamales with chicken. The father has made me like a representative of the women, so that, for example, with the women who sell food at church, I am in charge of keeping everything in order. And when we want to give something back to the church, because the father has given us so much, the best thing we can give is our own work.

As in churches throughout the United States, the parish priest has been a one-man first-response team to the immigrants his congregations serves. Rather than fight a losing battle against the changing demographics of Staten Island, the priest—who needed no census to tell him that the Mexican population of New York's boroughs had been exploding since the early 1990's—sought to bring the new community into his church.

PATRICIA: The father is American, but he speaks really good Spanish. We see him not just as a priest, but as more. Sometimes it's so difficult because our loved ones die in Mexico, and we need a lot of moral support. A year ago, my father died. You never get to see your loved ones again. Coming to the United States, achieving the American dream, costs a lot of tears and a lot of pain. But God rewards his children.

The rewards, slowly but surely, are beginning to arrive. Patricia's daughter attends college in New York City. The family's economic situation has stabilized, and they have rented a small house for the last seven years. English has not come easily to Patricia, who has invested more than a thousand dollars in books and videos to teach herself the language. "I would like to be able to communicate with people," she explains. Sometimes she asks her bilingual children to speak to her in English so she can practice. "Even in Mexico," she recalls, "I always dreamed of learning English."

But one crushing day in 2000 made it clear to Patricia that she had not yet "made it." Without a green card, she became forced to betray her most central value—her dedication to her family. When her father died suddenly in Mexico, Patricia was unwilling to risk the dangerous reentry into the United States, and could not leave the country to attend his funeral. If it were not for the support of the church, she says, she might have gone insane.

> PATRICIA: It was fatal for me, that he had died so suddenly. The father came, and he said, "No, Patricia, don't go. Believe me that if this were about money, I would find you the money. But I know that's not the only thing you need. You are not going to see your father, nor is he going to see you. So, we can pray for him, but we don't want to be worried about you." I was so sad, but I felt his moral support, that he was with us. I always said, "Why does the father care so much about us?" Everyone we know here on the Island came to our house, and we were praying for my father to rest in peace. My mother-in-law died also, and my husband couldn't go to the funeral either. He lost his mother and I lost my father. I feel like I am in a cage. But everyone has supported us. Getting involved in a church is really a great help.

For Patricia, the green card, the "papers," the detail, has been both inconsequential and crucial. "As my husband says, 'It's as if the papers were going to work,'" Patricia laughs. "But the one who does the work is me." And until the papers come, Patricia and Antonio will keep striving to achieve their goals without them.

PATRICIA: We have started our life, step by step, and it has taken a lot of effort. But we have achieved some triumphs that are like dreams to us, things we thought were out of reach because we don't have papers. But sometimes God has looked on us with merciful eyes. And there are people that have been able to help us, like the priest, for example. He has helped out all the immigrants here.

Zejaria Ozeri, a Mexican Jewish American

For about five hundred families in San Diego, staying in touch with their Mexican culture is the key to preserving their religion...their Jewish religion. Zejaria Ozeri, known as "Zeji" (pronounced "Zeh-chi") to his friends, has been community director, music teacher, theater troupe organizer and youth leader to San Diego's growing Mexican Jewish community. As he discusses his past while sipping coffee in a San Diego-area Starbucks, Zeji seems to know every other customer who walks through the doors. He kisses hello and discusses the latest developments of the local Jewish school in rapid Spanish. Like Enedino Aquino, Zeji's religious world is distinctly Mexican—and that is how Zeji likes it.

The son of an Israeli-born Yemenite Jew and a Mexican-born Russian Jew, Zeji was raised in the Jewish schools and youth movements of Mexico's 50,000 strong Jewish community[4]. As the son and grandson of immigrants to Mexico, migration never seemed out of the ordinary to Zeji.

ZEJI: After Europe, a lot of Jews arrived in Mexico hoping they would later get into the United States. So, we always lived with one foot in and another foot out—the feeling that at any moment we could be kicked out. We have this trauma that throughout history they have kicked us out. I think it's within the psyche of the Mexican Jew to be moving around. But I never saw any big problem. The truth is that Mexico, for the Jews, is a really good country.

At the age of eighteen, Zeji left Mexico to study theater in Israel, then joined an uncle in Los Angeles. A friend's brother lived in San Diego and invited Zeji down for a weekend. The friend took him to a party, and the moment Zeji entered the gathering, he discovered he knew everyone there. Classmates from the Jewish school he had attended in Mexico City, even his own first cousins whom he had not seen in nearly a decade, greeted him with hugs and kisses. "How on earth did all these Mexicans Jews get *here?*" he wondered.

Zeji loved it instantly. He began to play guitar for the guests at the party, and by the end of the night had received an offer to be a music teacher at a Mexican Jewish summer camp in San Diego.

> ZEJI: The nice thing about San Diego is that I am in the United States and in Mexico at the same time. The funny thing is that when they gave me my green card, the first thing I did was go to Mexico. Because finally, I could come and go as I pleased. And I wanted to go to Tijuana.

Originally in the country as a tourist, Zeji became a legal resident under special provisions for "religious workers." The Kent community center, around which Mexican Jewish life of San Diego revolves, has a new director now, but Zeji used to be the one running the show. "It is a place for kids to grow up and not lose their Jewish-Mexican values, their language, family, tradition, common history, and relationship with Israel. And they do not forget that they are Mexican."

He led youth activities, organized conferences, summer camps, groups for recently married couples, and even a soccer league. Every year, the center sends a group to the international Jewish dance festival in Mexico City. Zeji ran a Jewish-Mexican theater troupe, which traveled around California representing Mexico on some occasions, and the Jewish community on others. Although Zeji, like most San Diego-Mexican Jews, is bilingual, communal life takes place in Spanish.

Now a music teacher at a Jewish day school, Zeji has a lot of American Jewish coworkers, but his social world is still Mexican. "I don't have anything against the Americans," he explains. " It's just easier to click with Latinos."

> ZEJI: The problem is making friends in the U.S. People are difficult, and cold. In Mexico you have a friend to play tennis, soccer,

basketball, talk, eat, have dinner. Here, no. Here you have the soccer friend, or the drinks friend. The soccer friend wouldn't have dinner at your house, you only call him to play soccer. Isn't that really strange? But it's not like that with my Mexican friends. I call, "Are you at home? Yes? I'm coming over." With Americans, it's "What are you going to be doing on Thursday, November 27?" Give me a break!

San Diego's Mexican Jews, almost all of whom are professionals, according to the Jews themselves, might be viewed by outsiders as having more in common with American-born San Diego Jews than with other first-generation Mexican immigrants. Nearly all hail from Mexico City and the state of Nuevo León, while most Mexican immigrants continue to come from rural areas (although research shows that more and more immigrants are now coming from urban settings). Most Mexican Jews were upper-middle class or wealthy back in Mexico; most other Mexican immigrants were middle-class or poor. Yet, as Zeji tells it, life in the United States has put a new spin on the community's idea of belonging.

ZEJI: In the Jewish Community Center, the people who do the cleaning are Mexican. We have our Saturday activities there, and we have a really good relationship with the people who clean. Some Americans treat them only like employees who clean, but we treat them like human beings. This is what they do for a living, but they have relationships with the kids, and with us. Maybe in Mexico they wouldn't have paid attention to us because they are lower-middle class and we are upper-middle class. But here, that difference is broken because we are all here for the same reason. Our treatment is better, friendlier. More Latino.

Though he is the child and grandchild of immigrants to Mexico, Zeji identifies himself strongly as a Mexican—perhaps more strongly now than he did when he lived there. Living with "the best of both worlds" on the San Diego-Tijuana border, he is unsure whether his future will ever take him back to Mexico. But wherever Zeji decides to reside physically, his internal world remains in Mexico.

ZEJI: I would always consider that Mexico is my home. I was born there. I originally met a lot of my friends who live here in Mexico. School is there; Mexico Park is there, where I went walking for all of my childhood. I miss Mexico. I mean, in the university, you could be there two days and you already had friends. In Israel it's a little more difficult. It was easier with Latino people. I really like the humor, the soccer. The Mexican culture is really rich. Every state has its food, its traditions; the country is beautiful, and, in general, the people are good.

Yet, Zeji plans to become a U.S. citizen as soon as he is eligible. Many have romanticized the meaning of citizenship to those who choose to obtain it, claiming that emotional and patriotic reasons must be behind the decision to naturalize. As Zeji points out, however, his family's history suggests something different. Like his grandparents before him, he evaluates the question in very basic terms of personal and communal security. For Jews, he says, passports and affiliations can come to be matters of life and death.

ZEJI: I want to be an American because of the very same Jewish trauma. Here we are Mexicans, and you never know when they will change the laws. Laws are made—and changed—by men. I would like to become an American citizen now that I can have two nationalities. I wouldn't want to stop being a Mexican. I want to have the two nationalities because tomorrow, I don't want them to say, "Guess what, now only the Americans can stay, and the rest of you have two months to get out." But it's not because I *am* American. My kids will be Americans. But I think like a Mexican. There are different family values—I'm not saying better or worse—but different. And even more so as a Mexican Jew. In Jewish history, there have been a lot of surprises.

Part 4:

Building the United States

Some people come to Las Vegas for the night life, others for the gambling. Some come on vacation, others to retire. Benardo came to build.

As the hotel industry has boomed in Las Vegas, construction workers like Bernardo have been urgently needed to build hotels and restaurants, as well as the homes, apartments, and schools of the army of tourism industry workers that have flocked to the region.

Demand has been so great, in fact, that in spite of the challenges of being undocumented, Bernardo has several dozen other immigrants working for him on construction projects.

The New Pioneers

When the great railroads to California were built, much of the labor needed to complete them was provided by Chinese immigrants.[1] Indeed, they were the pioneers of their day, building on the frontiers of the emergent American nation. Today, I believe Mexican immigrants are the *new* pioneers—but the frontiers are not what they once were.

The new frontiers are the cities being redeveloped, the suburbs being built and the leisure destinations catering to an ever-wealthier America. Bernardo's experience of sudden success in the building industry of Las Vegas illustrates the great demand for building labor in the nation's holiday capital. In the nation's political capital, too, Mexican labor is building. In the suburbs of Washington, D.C., day laborer Gerardo is one of thousands of Latino laborers who refurbish, renovate, and rebuild the infrastructure surrounding the nation's capital.

That first-generation Mexican immigrants also engage in the intellectual work of building might surprise many, since the popular conception of Mexican immigrants is that they arrive completely uneducated. Yet, sixty-six percent of Mexicans who currently live in the United States have finished at least twelve years of schooling,[2] making them more educated than the general Mexican population. Though better known for filling the slots at the bottom of the labor market than those at the top, Mexican migrants count among their numbers thousands of high-tech emigrants. Whether these individuals have caused a "brain drain" in Mexico remains in debate, but what is certain is that they have been a "brain gain" for the United States.

The "land of opportunity" is constantly building and rebuilding, making and remaking itself, and it needs both the arms and the ingenuity of new immigrants to do so. Whether building hotels in Las Vegas and suburbs in Maryland or engineering the flows of information and products, Mexican immigrants have become the new American pioneers.

Bernardo, the Las Vegas Builder

"Everything was good," says Bernardo about the town of his birth, Zihuatlán, Jalisco. "But," he adds from his seat in a Las Vegas McDonald's, "it's everyone's dream to come here. One of my brothers came, then the next. Soon, we all started coming!" While others in his town had family members in the United States and had dreamed of migrating since they were children, Bernardo was the son of a reasonably successful fruit salesman. He says he did not start thinking about it until he was eighteen.

In 1986, the newly married Bernardo crossed the border illegally and began working in California. A year later, he returned to Zihuatlán, hoping his savings would fund a small business back home. Putting his dollars to work as pesos, he wanted to provide a better life for his family without leaving Mexico. But without the expertise to make the business a success, Bernardo soon found himself crossing the border once more, this time with his wife. On his first attempt, he was caught and put in a detention center where "the truth is, they didn't treat us badly." The next day, they tried again and made it across stuffed under the seats of a van. Ten others suffered the claustrophobic ride along with him.

Bernardo spent a few years doing migrant farm work in California and Washington before moving to Indio, a growing city in the desert a few hours drive east of Los Angeles. That was when Bernardo began to build the United States, doing roofing and carpentry for a contractor who also came from Zihuatlán.

But Bernardo says he always wanted more. He wanted to establish himself, to advance in his career, and he knew the only way would be with the coveted "green card." So in 1988, he acquired a false letter claiming that he had been a farm worker during the early 1980's. With this letter, he received amnesty under the 1985 provisions and became a legal resident of the United States.

For Bernardo, legal residency was the key to establishing a life in California. He continued working in carpentry and contracting and purchased a house. In 1993, as the United States recovered from recession and hotels started going up like wildfire in the fantasyland of Las Vegas, Bernardo and his wife divorced. "I wasn't happy in Indio" anymore, he says. "I felt sad in my house; I felt sad everywhere. My boss from Indio invited me to come work for him in Las Vegas. So in 1995, I did."

In the divorce, Bernardo got custody of his young daughter so he took her with him to Las Vegas. As demand for building increased and his days filled up with work, Bernardo found the challenges of single fatherhood to be great.

BERNARDO: I would take my daughter to school and then go to work. I would wait for her after school, and sometimes take her to the worksites with me. She would wait in the car if I didn't have anyone who could watch her. It was difficult, but I liked it. I liked it when it was the two of us. I would comb her hair, I would cook her food—well, bad food, but…I had to do a lot of things I wasn't accustomed to doing. But I really liked it because she's my daughter, and we were getting ahead in spite of everything.

Las Vegas gave Bernardo opportunities not just to work, but to learn as well. Although he had spent nearly a decade in California before coming to Nevada, it was in Vegas that he first learned English. "In California," he explains, "I worked with Hispanics. Everyone was Hispanic; everyone spoke Spanish. Here in Las Vegas, I started to work with Americans."

Just as legal residency allowed Bernardo a stronger foothold in Las Vegas, so the ability to cross the border freely permitted stronger ties with Zihuatlán. Shortly after divorcing, he met a woman on a trip to Zihuatlán and married her. As time went by, he brought brothers and sisters up to Las Vegas as well. "We would all contribute to the cost," he recalls. "We'd work together to bring one and then another. And now, we're all here." Of Bernardo's seven sib-lings, six now live in Las Vegas.

In 1996, however, the freedom he had come to cherish was sud-denly taken away. Auditing its records from the amnesty of the eighties, the INS asked for more proof of his supposed time as a farm laborer. Bernardo could produce none. He lost his green card. Once again, he was an undocumented immigrant.

> BERNARDO: It was very traumatic because when I had papers, I went to Mexico at Christmas and New Years, or on my parents' birthdays. The moment I lost my papers, everything changed. I can't leave because now I am afraid that the INS will catch me and put me in jail. Yeah, the one thing that changed was not being able to visit Mexico, but outside of that, I move around the United States without a problem…with absolutely no problem.

Still possessing a valid Social Security number, Bernardo reports his income each year. To the IRS, Bernardo is a successful contrac-tor who pays thousands of dollars annually in taxes; to the INS, he does not exist within the United States' borders.

Eventually, however, Bernardo learned that even the lack of legal papers was not an obstacle too great to overcome. Although he can no longer fly into the United States for lack of legal docu-ments, he says he has no problem crossing by land. "I walk across the line," he says, "and since I speak English they let me cross. They ask you how many stars the American flag has, and they let you cross."

In the end, economics proved to be more durable than borders for Bernardo. Even after his green card was taken away, the building boom in Las Vegas sent his career shooting up as fast as a new casino elevator.

> BERNARDO: My boss returned to Indio, but I stayed here. I began to work by the hour and taught myself the job. I got a work group together with four other guys, and little by little I got work. One company called me and then another, and I started to hire more

people. There have been times when I have had sixty people working for me. The least I have had is twenty. I worked on some famous hotels and maybe 2,000 apartments.

Like thousands of other immigrants—the last census counted 300,000 Hispanics in Las Vegas's Clark County— Bernardo thinks living standards are better in Vegas than they are in California. Rent is cheaper, he says, and the pay in the construction industry is good. The Hispanic community has grown noticeably since his arrival. While certain neighborhoods have attracted immigrants more than others, "Wherever you go, you'll see Hispanics. There are a lot of Hispanics working. Most of the Americans are managers, not laborers. The laborers are Hispanics, not anyone else."

BERNARDO: When the tourist comes, he spends money, so the city is growing. The city is becoming more prosperous. There are more casinos, there's more work. Then more people buy houses because they come to live here. Then you also have to build gas stations, shopping centers, more McDonald's. And it's important to emphasize that nothing gets done without Hispanic labor. Everywhere you go, the workers are Hispanic. But people don't see that. They see that there are some people who receive unemployment, or food stamps. But they don't pay attention to everything the Hispanic contributes. We also pay our taxes, we pay the same taxes as an American but we do the most difficult kind of work.

But things will surely be better for his kids, says Bernardo. Born in the United States, they will have more opportunities than their undocumented father. The daughter from his first marriage now lives with her mother in Seattle. Bernardo misses her in Las Vegas, but feels confident that she is on the right track. "She likes school and sports," he says, "and she is bilingual. She's a normal kid. The divorce didn't really affect her that much."

She wants to be a doctor, "and with everything I have, I am going to support and help her."

His decades in the United States have politicized Bernardo some-
what. He thinks his construction work is important for Las Vegas'
economy, and he hopes some day that his adopted country will
reward his work with legal papers once more.

> BERNARDO: What more can a person want than for the border to
> disappear? For it to be easier for the people that do work to re-
> ceive a work permit? These are people who report their taxes,
> who don't have problems with the police, with drugs, with drink-
> ing, with none of that.

Bernardo says he lives a quiet life of work and family. New car, new
house, kids in private schools—other than the "detail" of his green
card, he has made it. When relatives come to visit, he takes them
out to shows on the strip. But even though he builds casinos,
Bernardo is not one to spend time in them. "I like to go have break-
fast there," he explains. "I like to go to the restaurants. But play?
No, I don't really like to play."

Gerardo, the Day Laborer

The day Gerardo fell from a ladder and dislocated three discs in his back, his "day labor" income did not even amount to an honest day's pay.

GERARDO: There are many times that they just don't pay me, that they trick me. And we can't say anything. Once, while painting a house, I fell from a ladder and hurt myself. I went to some lawyers, and they were handling my case. To this day, I have pain. I was seeing a doctor, and they sent me to a clinic in Washington. They told me I had two or three discs out of place, because they always hurt and I can't move. But the lawyers said there was no point to continue my case, that the company was never going to pay anything. They never even paid me for that day of work.

In this Maryland suburb of the nation's capital, immigrants— most of them Central American—gather each morning at a day labor center. As the needs of the construction industry twist and bend from one day to the next, day labor must twist and bend with them. What this means for day laborers, however, is that it is easier for an employer to break their end of the bargain.

GERARDO: It happens a lot that I don't get paid, but what can we do to them? We have to keep moving on because if you become someone's enemy, you can't live. You know you can't do anything because you are a foreigner. They take us to work and say we will do one thing, but then they give us another. Once they took us to work, me and another guy, and we finished the work at 4 p.m. but they didn't come to pick us up until 11 p.m. The owners of the house were Black, and thank goodness they were Christians—they gave us food to eat because we had no food. And they said, "Look, if the man doesn't come, you can sleep in the garage."

For Coatzacoalcos, Veracruz native Gerardo, even a Washington, D.C. garage would have been a step up from the conditions in which he lived prior to migration. He and his wife did not have a house, but rather, lived in a shack of corrugated cardboard and wooden boards. When the "Norte" wind swept into Veracruz from the Gulf of Mexico, it would thrash the dwelling and tear it apart.

> GERARDO: Since my father liked to work a lot, we were okay. Not very well-off, but as we say, there was food on the table. My parents went to work at three in the morning to sell things at the *mercado*, the market, and returned at two in the afternoon. They were able to give us good food to eat. But when they took the *mercado* down, there was no money. My father just went out to fish, to harvest crabs and shrimp to sell to the cantinas. My brothers were older and I was still young, but I was already working. At eight years old, I began to work.

In Coatzacoalcos, Gerardo grew up and married. Sometimes, he says, there was enough to eat, and sometimes there was not. Those were the times that his brother-in-laws would call from Maryland, asking, "Why don't you come up here?"

> GERARDO: I told him, "How? We have never traveled there. We have seen airplanes, but only as they pass up above in the sky. I asked my wife, "Why would we go there if we are just going to suffer even more? We don't speak English; we don't know anyone. Why would I go to work there?"

And yet, in one sudden decision, Gerardo decided he and his wife would cross. He called his brothers-in-law and asked them to wire the money to Tijuana, and the couple set off for the border. When they got there, they collected the money—enough for everything: hotel, bus, food, and of course, the coyote's fee to actually cross the line.

Upon arrival in this Maryland suburb of Washington, D.C., Gerardo immediately began working as a painter's assistant. His wife sold tamales, and within a few months, the couple sent for the kids. That was nine years ago.

> GERARDO: Today I am a professional painter. I know paint, and I know my work. Even though I don't speak English, people al-

ways like my work. So far, we haven't been able to get papers. A few days ago I was working in a company, and the man told me he had to take out money to pay taxes. He took the money out, but I can't file because I don't have a legal number. Right now, I don't have a fixed job. I come here to find work. Sometimes I work, sometimes I don't.

Gerardo paints mostly homes and apartment buildings, he says, proudly carrying his box of tools and brushes. He says he would like to have a steadier job. He would like to file his taxes. But he cannot do any of these things without legal papers. Gerardo, in spite of his undocumented status, wants to play by the rules.

GERARDO: It's a crime, and if they find out we have false papers, it will be a huge problem. Maybe that is going to be fixed now, but what I hear in the news is that it will only be for people who have filed their taxes. So we, well, we also pay taxes because we pay rent, we pay so many things, we go shopping and they charge us the taxes and if we go to work in a company for a day, they take out taxes and all of this money goes to the government.

As day laborers, Gerardo and the other Latino immigrants who line up with him in the morning are the most vulnerable workers in the building trades. For Gerardo, time and again employers have little incentive to make good on their promises. The only sanction the workers have at their disposal is word of mouth—an employer who does not pay his worker finds it difficult to continue hiring workers at the same day labor center. Center staff keeps a log of which laborer has gone with which employer, and how much is agreed for payment. This, says Gerardo, increases the likelihood that the workers will get paid. But it is no guarantee. Even more common, he says, is trickery and cheating.

GERARDO: They pay us with checks, and the company says that it has to pay its taxes, so they take out taxes. One company hired me for $14 an hour. I worked for nine hours and they only gave me $50.

The game is the same, day in and day out. The day of this interview, Gerardo awoke at 4:30 a.m. to line up at the day labor center. He says he earns about $700-800 a month. Life is not punctuated by visits to the family in Mexico— since Gerardo is undocumented, he cannot take the risk.

> GERARDO: Sometimes it's difficult to work so hard. You have to work, and I work on ladders and sometimes I don't want to do it. But what can I do? I have to do it. My wife has also been sick. Maybe we will return to Mexico next year.

Although employers often treat his labor as if it is worthless, Gerardo has developed a consciousness of what his own work and the work of other Latinos is really worth, and the ways in which they are changing the United States. "The Hispanics," he says, "are spread out through all the country. Wherever you go, there they are…working."

1   Ronald Takaki, A *Different Mirror: a history of multicultural America* (New York: Back Bay Books, 1993).

2   Conapo, Census 2002

Part 5:

Still "In" Mexico

On a gray day in Elgin, Illinois, sixty-seven year old Alfonso Martínez squints his clear, gray-blue eyes against the wind. He is ready to leave the cold behind and go back to Mexico. He is ready to cash in on the only investment his years of work in the United States have reaped—the education of his kids.

Can You Go Home Again?

The idea that immigrants who come to the United States from around the world break ties entirely with their countries of origin has persisted in popular imagination, even though the reality of that idea has diminished with each passing year. It seems to me that of all the American immigration myths, perhaps this one has been the slowest to die.

As many correctly point out, the Mexican case does have its differences, as the stories of my binational childhood illustrate. When "home" is just over the border, keeping in touch and participating in the country of origin is easier than it would be across oceans and continents. Still, in some ways Mexicans historically have participated *less* in the political and economic lives of their homeland than other immigrant groups. Diaspora Jews long have focused their political and economic capital on the building of Israel; Croatians and Armenians in the United States were largely responsible for the dramatic reemergence of these two countries in the last decade, and Indians abroad send back the money that keeps their families afloat.

Although Mexicans remain physically close to Mexico, many Mexicans abroad have been wary of participating or investing in the country our families had left. After all, the same party had ruled for seventy-one years, and many felt Mexico had failed our families. By failing to provide them with economic opportunities, Mexico forced them to risk their lives crossing the border to thankless jobs in the United States. Corruption, many felt, had robbed their communities of the chance to become more prosperous. And prior to 2000, the lack of democracy and prospects for change did not allow for even the hope that things might improve in the near future.

There was one thing, however, which Mexico's emigrants never stopped believing in—their families. Family remittances, more than any other aspect of immigrant participation in Mexico, have changed the face of the country. From 1996-2001 alone, Mexicans abroad sent more than $36 billion home to their families! Each year saw an increase from the year before, with $9 billion entering in 2001.[1] Mexican authorities calculate that in 2005, Mexicans abroad may send as much as $20 billion home. Some economists indicate that every "migra-dollar" that enters Mexico raises economic production in Mexico by three times, because these dollars are spent either on investment or on consumption, which in turn stimulates production.[2] These dollars are also invested in the education of children and relatives.

In the past decade, the traditional attitude of Mexican emigrants has started to change, and the contributions of Mexicans abroad to our countries and communities of origin have increased dramatically. Some, have become successful in the United States, taking advantage of their familiarity with Mexico to do business with their home communities. Others, like Tereso Ortiz, have founded clubs and federations to build public works projects in the communities back home. And, a significant group of migrants have gone back to Mexico to get involved in politics. In traditional migrant-sending states like Zacatecas, Guanajuato and Jalisco, migrant-mayors have become regular fixtures. After all, Mexican migrants have the opportunity to witness a new kind of politics in the United States—a robust political system and civil society. "Returning" to Mexico to change things back home, whether physically or psychologically, has for many been the next logical step.

Tereso Ortiz, the Guanajuato Connection

Every day "Don Tereso," as Dallas' Mexican community knows Tereso Ortiz, wakes up at 5 a.m. to begin his day as a manager at a cement factory. At 5 p.m. he arrives at Casa Guanajuato, where he stays until nine or ten at night receiving phone calls from Mexicans in need of assistance, organizing community events, talking with officials from his home town of Ocampo and supervising Casa Guanajuato activities like boxing lessons and beauty pageants. Tereso thinks these activities will help kids stay connected to Mexico. His passion for serving the town and state of his birth has brought thousands together in Dallas, for the sake of community and for the love of Guanajuato.

Tereso, the fifth of sixteen siblings, was born in Ocampo, Guanajuato in 1949. Ocampo, he explains, "is one of those pueblos that has more people in Dallas than in Ocampo! Of all the pueblos in Mexico, it has one of the largest percentages in the United States." Whatever the source of his statistics, there is no doubt that Ocampenses are as much of a presence in Dallas as they are in Ocampo—and that Guanajuatenses remain among the best-organized Mexicans in Dallas.

Tereso first made the trip to the United States when he was twenty-one years old and a newlywed. By then, a decade had already passed since he'd left school to help his parents in the fields. "I can speak of very simple things about the area where we lived," says the mild-mannered Tereso, as the sound of a boxing match thumped on the television in the next room.

TERESO: I saw that in my pueblo there was not much work. I felt that it was the moment to do something for my future. I discussed it with my wife, and we reached an agreement. We had been married for just six months, and I decided to come to the United States to seek a better life. I was working in the fields with my father, but I wanted to progress. So in May of '71 I crossed to this side. Thank God it turned out well. We arrived around two in the afternoon, on the seventh or so of May. And, as I sometimes say to my friends, I arrived at 2 p.m., and by 4 p.m. I had already found work.

Working in a Dallas-area restaurant and then switching to a vegetable-packing plant, Tereso sent money home and did his best to save. "Naturally," he says, he missed his wife and family, and a year and a half later he returned to Ocampo.

Back in Ocampo, Tereso tried very hard to make staying there economically possible. He had returned with twenty thousand pesos, and used them to open a shoe store, bringing employment to his family and shoes to his marginalized town.

TERESO: I opened a store and sold shoes. It was going well. Every Friday, I would go to the city of León to buy shoes. It's far away, and at that time there was no direct highway, so I went by bus. I felt that the store was going well, but I had to spend the day every Friday to go buy the merchandise in León. So I said, "What's missing? A vehicle." I spoke with my father and said, "Look, I would like a car, but here we can't buy one. What do you think about me going north again, so we can buy the car?"

Leaving the shoe store in his father's care, Tereso returned to the United States. "To this day," he says, "I still haven't taken that car."

Arriving back in Dallas, Tereso started working in a warehouse and quickly rose through the ranks to become its assistant manager. Things were going well at work, and Tereso began to think his stay in Dallas would be more than temporary. He called his wife and asked her and their young child to join him. Two weeks after arriving, she gave birth to the couple's second child—an American citizen.

As he became more established in Dallas, surrounded by other Ocampenses, Tereso remained concerned about the town he had left behind.

> TERESO: I received a letter from the parish. And in this letter, the priest, Mr. Isidro Mendez—I remember his name—told us three things: Wherever you are, don't forget where you come from. Don't forget your roots; don't forget your traditions. Don't forget your culture. I think that was really important for me, and was the inspiration for the things I do for the organizations, especially with Casa Guanajuato. It's the idea that we need to think a little about how to transmit the incredibly beautiful tradition that we have in pueblos like mine.

The most important day of the year in Ocampo is June 24, the birthday of the pueblo's patron saint, San Juan Bautista. Ocampenses in Dallas celebrate it, too, and whenever possible, take their kids to Mexico to see the real thing. In 1975, Tereso and friends formed the United Brotherhood of Ocampo, originally to raise money to contribute flowers or music to the annual fiesta "back home." The needs in Ocampo were innumerable, and the Brotherhood of Ocampo in Dallas tried to help their families meet them.

> TERESO: In Ocampo there are old people who don't have anything to cover themselves with in December when it's very cold. So we said, "Let's get together some money to send them blankets." Then the parish said, "Look, we are going to buy a new church bell. What do you think?" Why not? So we have a raffle, and we raise the amount to buy the things, and whatever is left over, we send for the yearly *fiesta* or to an emergency fund.

In the 1970's, as Tereso's group became successful and similar "hometown clubs" began springing up around the United States, particularly in New York, Chicago, Dallas, and Los Angeles. Today there are hundreds of them. Like Tereso's group, many started as social gatherings intent on sharing their hometown's important fiestas with their kids. But as migrants became more successful economically, these clubs began to tackle some of the development problems of their hometowns, building portable water pipes, reconstructing church pews and repaving plazas.

Mexico's government remained largely oblivious to these developments. It was not until 1994 that government officials started noticing the work of Tereso and his compatriots. First, the Mexican consul in Dallas started attending their events, then the state of Guanajuato started sending its representatives to see what their *paisanos* in Dallas were up to. Two decades after Tereso and friends formed their first association, the Guanajuato state government, seeing the potential in their work, started urging the various Dallas-area clubs of Guanajuatenses to form an association. Leaders like Tereso took the suggestion, and that same year Casa Guanajuato was born. Soon Mexican mayors, governors, and even presidential hopefuls began to visit Casa Guanajuato. (President Vicente Fox has visited this town-home association three times.)

TERESO: When Casa Guanajuato began, the first goal we set was to celebrate some of the fiestas that are popular in Mexico. The first fiesta we celebrated was Day of the Dead. My church, Santa Cecilia, gave us the opportunity to use their gym. We built an altar there, like a cultural representation with music, dance, and everything. I think there were about four hundred people at that activity. We realized that we were doing something really wonderful. Then came the twentieth of November, and we had a celebration of the Mexican Revolution. Then we realized that we needed a place of our own because we couldn't always ask the churches to give us space. We looked for a place for a month or two, and now here we are in Oak Cliff with our own building.

Casa Guanajuato is no longer just for Guanajuatenses; they now have their doors open to all Mexicans in Dallas and have sponsored pageants for the "Queen of the Fiesta" from cities in other Mexican states. Casa Guanajuato now has members numbering in the thousands—probably the most successful town-home association of its type in the U.S. Of Tereso's six children, five were born in the United States. But Tereso keeps looking back—back to

Ocampo, back to Mexico. If Mexico is changing—and he seems to think it is—Tereso wants to be a part of that change.

TERESO: With the elections in the year 2000 we had the opportunity to change Mexico. I don't have anything against any particular government, but the truth is that for us it used to be really sad and difficult. I have spent more than thirty years on this side and every time I go back to Mexico, I suffer a lot. But with all the changes in Mexico, I think we have the opportunity to take advantage of the doors that have been opened. I think it's really important that our kids participate, that they grow up in a Mexican environment. It's not that we don't want them to worry about the American side. It's important that they integrate with the American community. We are now U.S. citizens. But even those that are born in America should not forget where their roots are.

1 Banco de México.

2 Jorge Durand, Emilio Parrado and Douglas Massey. "Migradollars and Development: A Reconsideration of the Mexican Case." *International Migration Review* 3:2, 423-444.

Part 6:

In Defense of Each Other

Practicing the American Way

Migrants are among the most vulnerable human populations on earth. In a new land, knowing little to none of the language, unfamiliar with the environment, and oftentimes undocumented, migrants have been subject to abuse by unscrupulous employers and businesspeople. Historically they have been neglected by governments.

(See Appendix: Declaration of Migrant Rights and State Responsibilities.)

Yet, it seems to me that perhaps this is why immigrants have been some of the greatest advocates for social reform in the United States. In particular, they have sought to support and stand up for other members of their communities. In many instances, immigrants are the ones who have held the United States accountable for living up to its own promise — the ones who have improved the state of civil and human rights for all Americans.

One such change that immigrants have brought to U.S. society has been their struggle to improve labor conditions, largely through the building of unions and interest groups. In 1909 and 1920, Jewish immigrant garment workers went on strike for many of the things Americans now take for granted, such as fifty-hour weeks and overtime pay.

But the ethics of group service and protection among immigrants to the United States has hardly been limited to such grand expressions. As long as there have been immigrants, there have been immigrant advocates. Using no greater tool than their knowledge of English or the workings of U.S. society, they have tried to get a better deal for their fellow immigrants.

The undocumented status of millions of modern-day immigrants has served to keep immigrants quiet on many counts. Yet, what I have seen in my travels throughout the United States is that Mexican immigrants have found ways to work around this. Even the undocumented have found their own voice in recent decades. The results of their struggles are creating a better society—ironically perhaps, a society *more* ruled by law and order—than that to which they arrived.

For Mexican immigrants trying to change the society around them, lack of legal documents may be less of an obstacle than lack of English skills. Thus, those who speak English become the interlocutors and the defenders of other Mexican immigrants, helping them negotiate with the English-speaking society that surrounds them. Julio advocates for his fellow Mexican immigrants on a regular basis in Wimberley, Texas. Though he has no legal documents, his English skills and gentle manner allow him to alert local authorities to injustices committed against the Mexicans of Wimberley.

Lorena, on the other hand, wants to change the process itself. She leads Mexican immigrants in public actions trying to obtain amnesty. The possibility that she could become a citizen of a country where citizens have the power to change things is too great a promise for her to let go unfulfilled.

Julio, the Protector

Julio tries not to think about what would have happened if Sam Jones had been carrying a gun that day. Speaking English and being on good terms with the elderly people whose odd jobs he does in Wimberley, Texas, Julio had become a local advocate for his fellow Mexicans. He had never thought that confrontation with a drunk like Sam Jones would be part of the deal.

A friend of Julio's had confided that a boss named Sam Jones owed him $5000 in back pay. Julio knew one of his bosses was friends with the town judge, and after telling the boss what had happened, the boss approached the judge about the issue. The judge, in turn, called Jones, but he claimed he did not owe any money to anyone. Finally, he offered $2000, and on the judge's advice, Julio's friend took it.

JULIO: But then, Sam Jones found me in town. He followed my truck while I was dropping a friend off at his house. Sam Jones had another person in the car with him, and he followed me. I said to myself, "Oh, God, what am I going to do?" There was nowhere to turn around. So Jones parked behind my truck. He came to my car door, and I locked it. His friend went to the other door. Jones put his face to the window and said, "You know what? You are getting yourself involved in a lot of things that have nothing to do with you!" So I said, "Yes, it does have to do with me." And he said, "Get out of the car! Get out!" And he started swearing at me in English, but I understand English! I said, "You can break the glass if you want, but I'm not going to get out of the car." He was drunk. I could smell the liquor. So my friend said to Sam Jones, "This is my house. Get out of here. If you have problems with Julio, deal with them somewhere else. I don't want problems." So Jones understood that he was on someone else's property, and he left.

Julio did not see Sam Jones again for four months, and when finally the two did run into each other, Jones acted as though nothing at all had happened. Julio, however, did not forget so easily. "Sometimes it depresses me," he says, "that in order to help someone else, you put yourself in danger. Just imagine what would have happened if he had a gun with him, or if he had punched me. He was drunk."

Though still undocumented, Julio is bilingual and counts dozens of native-born Americans among his friends, and this places him closer to people with influence than most others in this town's small Mexican community. Using that influence to protect others has been his most natural instinct.

Largely, this is because he has been in town longer than most. One of twelve siblings, Julio left his hometown of Dolores Hidalgo, Guanajuato more than a decade ago. "Sometimes it didn't rain there," he says, "and I saw that we were really suffering. So I decided to come to the United States."

An uncle and a cousin were already in Texas, and Julio joined them in Austin. He worked three months as a construction assistant, but never saw a penny for his work. Then, the cousin met a man from Wimberley, a small town of just under 4,000 people in the hill country surrounding Austin, who was asking around for a worker who could come to Wimberley to help out on his ranch. Julio and Paul Petersen met, and Julio was off to Wimberley.

Paul Petersen had traveled throughout Mexico and spoke Spanish. A good thing, says Julio, because as a recent arrival, he spoke no English. Julio lived on the Petersen's ranch and worked for five years, interrupted only by Christmas visits to his family in Mexico.

> JULIO: I realized that I was traveling a lot to Mexico and putting my life at risk—a snake on the path, or the river, or something. I saw that it was really dangerous, and that a lot of people died. So I decided to bring my wife and kids—at that time we had three kids, and then one was born here. They came here in 1990, and our youngest was born in 1992. I decided that here there was a better future for the kids.

At first, Julio and his wife could not even read simple papers the school sent them, and their children had to translate. Then Julio decided that learning English should be a priority. Though he did this interview in Spanish, he is fully functional in English as well.

> JULIO: I tell the young guys they should study English. And they say, "I don't like English." I tell them, "Look, I learned English, not because I liked it, but because I needed it. People ask me to come to the doctor with them to translate, or to do the registration of their car, or something. I saw that I needed to learn English. So I went to school for three years, and I used cassettes, and I spoke a lot of English with my kids. They taught me a lot of English. I say it's important, because if we live in this country it's important to learn the language. When people come here for the first time, I tell them, "You know what? The first step is to learn English. You need it now and in the future."

It was English, in fact, that allowed Julio to find better paying work after five years with "Pablo Petersen." He makes $9 an hour as an aide to elderly people in town. Each day of the week he has a different regular client. "I like my work," he says, "Because I'm not just doing one thing. I do lots of different things, a little of this and a little of that." Sometimes he gets calls from others wanting his services. "I tell them, 'Yes, but I'm already full.'" His wife works as a maid two or three days a week.

But Julio's workday goes beyond his paid employment. Always, it seems, there is a new arrival from Mexico in need of his advice and protection.

> JULIO: Yes, there are a lot of Mexicans. I think there are about three hundred of us. I know of lots of little ranches where four or five Mexicans live. I know a lot of people here. I know people from Oaxaca, Guerrero, Veracruz, San Luis Potosí, and Durango. There was this young man that I met, he was about fifteen. I invited him here to my house and helped him look for work. Really nice, this guy, a really good person. I asked him, "Why did you come here so young? You should have studied in Mexico to

arrive more prepared!" And he said, "No, I had to come because I am the oldest of the family, and there is no work there, so I had to come." He was here for two years. My wife gave him meals. And then he went to Dallas, and he is earning $16 an hour there! I try to help the young people more than anything. I don't want people to abuse them, because here there are a lot of abuses.

There is something very paternal about Julio. He thinks of himself as the collective dad of all the young Mexican immigrants whose paths cross his in their search for a better life. He gives them advice: Learn English. Ask for your salary at the end of every day. And if people give you problems and you need help, come to me.

His role as the father in his own family, too, defines his priorities more than anything else. It is because of his kids, he says, that he is absolutely certain he will never return to Mexico, even if he has to stay undocumented forever. His children are bilingual and advancing in school, and Julio says he will never take that opportunity from them.

JULIO: I don't forget about Mexico. I carry it in my heart always. Here I have my flag, see? It's my fatherland, it's where I was born; it's where I suffered, everything. And when I remember it I feel bad, and I want to cry because even after all the suffering I experienced there, it's my country. I ask God to help the people who are crossing the border, that they make it here, that they progress and that they work, because that is why they come. Sometimes my friends say to me, "You're not going back to Mexico?" And I tell them that maybe one day to visit, yes. But to live, no. Because I brought my family here with a dream, with a future. And if I return to Mexico, instead of living in the years 2010 or 2020, I would live in the eighties and nineties, I would be behind. I have nieces and nephews in Mexico that go to school, and the kids in sixth or seventh grade don't have computers in their schools. My son here just started second grade and he already knows how to use the computer.

Julio points to the computer he bought his children, on a small table in the family's small trailer. The trailer is parked on the ranch of one of his bosses, and with one day of work per week, Julio pays the utilities and the rent on the land. The boss bought the trailer, and Julio paid it off at $250 a month for three years. After his last payment, the landlord threw Julio a surprise party to celebrate. "He made a cake and he gave me this diploma," says Julio, proudly indicating the homemade "Certificate of Home Ownership" that sits on his shelf. "He said he was giving me the diploma because every month for three years, I paid the $250, and always on the fifteenth of the month."

"The Americans have good rules," says Julio. "I like their rules."

Lorena, the Immigrant Advocate

Lorena says she was never supposed to get this far. She was never even supposed to get to Mexico City, let alone the Bronx. But, she acknowledges, the easy way was never Lorena's way.

> LORENA: When I started wanting to learn how to read, I must have been thirteen or fourteen years old, and a friend started to teach me the vowels. But everything had to be hidden, because my aunt was very strict and she preferred for me to help her with housework. She said she never sent me to school because my father didn't want me to study. Back then, women didn't go to school, they just learned to do housework. Then, when I was fifteen years old, I left my aunt's house and went to work in the field with my father. We grew tomatoes, chiles, all kinds of vegetables.

From a young age, Lorena had lived with her aunt near the city of Izúcar de Matamoros, in the state of Puebla. Since the early 1980's, Puebla has been sending a steady stream of migrants to the New York area. Lorena was not allowed to set foot in a school classroom. But, she decided if she could not study, at least she wanted her brothers to be able to. So she convinced her father to let her go work in Mexico City, where she would send money back to help support her brothers' education. "Okay," he said to her. "If you want them to study, you're going to have to work for it."

Work for it Lorena did. She hired herself out as a full-time maid in Mexico City, and her earnings bought her brothers notebooks and pencils, school uniforms and shoes. In a town where most barely completed elementary school, one of Lorena's brothers completed high school and the other became a teacher.

But rather than return to her family after a few years, Lorena stayed on in Mexico City, where at the age of twenty-one, she met the man who was to become her husband. After dating for a year, Lorena was still scared to marry him "since my mom had lots of problems with my dad. And it's always scary to try to start a home." So the two moved in together without telling their parents. When Lorena became pregnant with their first child, they decided to marry. Lorena kept working as a maid and her husband as a messenger, and five years later they purchased a small house.

A lawyer at her husband's workplace offered him a job as a private chauffeur, ostensibly making the same money. But six months later the deal suddenly changed, and he was out of work. "My husband never again had a good job," says Lorena. "We still owed on part of the house, and we really went into debt." At this point, the couple was expecting their second child.

A brother of Lorena's was already in New York. In 1990, Lorena proposed to her husband that crossing over to join him would be a good way to help resolve the family's debt problems. Her husband was resistant to the idea, but said he would do it. "I said, 'Look, with two kids and debts, you can't just cross your arms and wait for something to happen,'" Lorena says. "You don't like it, but you have to do it."

Her husband agreed, and they made the journey. Within a year, his earnings had paid off their debts, and he asked his wife and kids to join him in the Bronx. Her husband's goal, she says, was to save enough money to return to Mexico and buy a taxi. Lorena, how-ever, had other plans.

LORENA: My idea was for my kids to learn a different language, other than Spanish. I saw a better future for my son and my daughter. It's easier to find work with two languages. If my husband saved his money and then wanted us to return, well, I would return with him, but maybe my kids would want to stay here. But he didn't find work that allowed him to save. He was earning $300 a week, and I was earning $200.

Her husband worked at an Italian restaurant, and Lorena at a cloth-ing factory. Factory conditions took their toll on her. She was not allowed to go to the bathroom during the workday, and felt that her managers treated her with too much disrespect. So she quit and started to work as a maid.

But three years ago, she started to get sick. It started with suspicious pains. Then, doctors administered a TB test, and told her she was particularly susceptible to the disease. Follow-up visits resulted in a medical prescription, and one month of medicine soon became nine. But she felt the medicine was only making her worse. In a year of treatments at a health clinic for the poor, she never saw the same physician twice. A different doctor diagnosed arthritis.

Unable to get out of bed for months, Lorena stopped work and has yet to return. There is still no clear diagnosis for her ailment.

Being bedridden did not suit Lorena. She began attending leadership courses with other Latino immigrant women. As undocumented workers' hopes for an amnesty rose over the summer of 2001, just months before the September 11 attacks, Lorena came out of bed to help organize marches. Unlike other immigrants who perceive their undocumented status as a minor detail, Lorena says she feels the weight of her green card's absence in every aspect of life. And this, she says, is what makes her angry enough to push her frail body into action.

> LORENA: We organize marches because we want an amnesty for immigrants. I call people, I invite them, I tell them we should go, that we should support the cause so we can have better jobs, a better life for ourselves and our kids. A lot of the people whose kids were born here are fine because their kids have their rights, even though their parents don't. But they have all the benefits, and my kids don't. There are a lot of people who don't have benefits, like me. Poor girls, poor guys. The girls get together with a guy because it's an illusion of happiness, because they wanted to work but they couldn't, they wanted to study but they couldn't. I have seen a lot, and I tell my husband we have to make the sacrifice now that we're here.

Life in the United States has taken its toll on her relationship with her husband, she says. She feels that he does not have the same drive she does—the same persistence, the same unwillingness to be defeated. The two often work opposite hours, and even when their time at home coincides, her husband is too exhausted to enjoy it with her.

Lorena herself may have been denied an education, but the couple is sacrificing to give one to their oldest daughter. She is now a student at a local public university, but as an undocumented immigrant she is not eligible for the discounted tuition rates offered to residents. Lorena's husband took out a loan from his employer to pay the $7,000 a year for their daughter's education.

Lorena herself still has not learned English, despite a brief stint in ESL night school. "I think my memory has not developed in this sense," she says. "It has developed only in work, work. What I will say is that even if I don't speak English, I do know how to work."

Part 7:

Getting Educated

Fulfilling the Dream

Some stories of immigrant mobility are based on the growth of a business, others are based on education. In the case of Mexican immigrants, we are more likely to hear the first story than the second.

Unfortunately, the popular idea that Mexican immigrants and Mexican-Americans have lower education levels than the general population are not without statistical support. In 1998, just ten percent of Hispanics aged twenty-five to twenty-nine held a bachelor's degree, a gap of twenty-two percentage points from the rate for non-Hispanic whites.[1]

Yet, I must point out something the thousands of Mexicans immigrants I have met have taught me, and which statistics collaborate—there is another side to the story. Indeed, that ten percent is double what the rate was in 1970. When the statistic is broken down into U.S.-born and foreign-born Hispanics, it becomes apparent the second generation is making educational strides beyond those of their parents. Only fifty percent of foreign-born Hispanics had high school diplomas in 1998, compared with eighty percent of U.S.-born Hispanics.[2]

Though the second generation tends to be more educated than the immigrant generation, in this section I want to point to two important realities that are often missed. First, education does not only "happen" to the second generation, but to the first generation as well. And second, bilingualism and biculturalism has shaped and sharpened the educations of Mexican immigrants. It has made them more, not less, capable of success in their academic and professional lives.

Luisa and Victor represent what many call the "half" generation. They came to the United States with their parents as young children. They have come up through the U.S. educational system, yet they are undocumented immigrants. Both want to attend college, but only Victor knows he will be able to do so. U.S. law requires states to educate all students through high school, regardless of migratory status. Yet, once the university years arrive, most students will be asked for their social security numbers. Traditionally, this has left the "half generation" of undocumented children with few options. They either must return to Mexico to solicit a "student visa" and return to pay international student tuition (an option most cannot afford), or leave their educations behind altogether. Many opponents of facilitating higher education for the undocumented suggest these students "go back to Mexico" to study, but in most cases, they do not want to leave their families in the United States, nor are they interested in starting anew in an educational system other than the only one they have ever known. Often, returning to Mexico is impossible, as many universities do not acknowledge diplomas from U.S. high schools.

In 2001, Texas became the first U.S. state (followed shortly by California) to allow migrant students who graduated from Texas high schools to attend state and community colleges, paying in-state tuition with no questions asked about their legal status. Thus, Victor is looking forward to a math major at a University of Texas campus.

Luisa, who has grown up in Georgia, does not have this security, as Georgia has no such law. She can only hope to convince university administrators that she is worth educating, or hope that by a stroke of luck, nobody will ask for her social security number at all.

Luisa, Hoping to Study

Whether Luisa will be able to attend college is not in her hands, but she is taking control over her community relations and her teeth. In the small Georgia town where she lives, the Mexican population has exploded in the last decade due to demand for labor in chicken plants. Luisa's mother spends her days in those plants, while Luisa completes her senior year in high school. She plays volleyball and works on the school newspaper, hoping her undocumented status will not prevent her from going to college to study computers. In the afternoons, she works three jobs to pay for her own braces, and on weekends she tries to make a good name for Mexican immigrants in the trailer park where she used to live.

Luisa came to Georgia when she was just seven years old, following her mother there from Obregón, Sonora. Soon, they sent for Luisa's younger sister to join them as well. Though Luisa claims to have loved "diagramming sentences" in junior high English classes, she seems most comfortable speaking Spanish, with some English mixed in. When she does speak English, her only accent is a Southern one.

When Luisa first arrived in Georgia, her family lived in a trailer park. They were the only Mexicans there, and as a young girl, Luisa already had put herself to the task of getting to know the neighbors.

> LUISA: Where I lived in the trailer, I have American friends. I get along really well with them. They love me and I love them. In fact, I'm going on vacation with them this Monday. We were the only Hispanics in the trailer park. They call me, I call them; I visit them, I go out to eat with them. I go to their house and we talk. They're like parents to me. They call me their daughter. They tell me to be careful, and they give me advice. They were the only neighbors we talked with, our neighbors on the right side. They had a bad impression of Hispanics before. You could

even say they were racists. But once they got to know me, they started to see that I didn't want to take anything away from them, that we only came for the work. They told me that they had another impression of us, and that with me they started to see I was not the kind of person they thought Hispanics were. I always tell them, "We come for the jobs. It's to have a better life." If we had everything they have, we wouldn't need to come!

Luisa says she likes the small-town environment because everyone knows everyone. "In Atlanta," she says, "people are much less likely to know one another." In the past decade, she has watched the Mexican population of her small Georgia town grow exponentially, mostly due to the demand for labor in the chicken plants. Though Hispanics are certainly a minority at her high school, she says their numbers have quadrupled since she started.

Community relations in town have been, by all accounts, mostly positive since the influx of Mexican immigrants began. Luisa is unfazed by the few incidents she has experienced. "Sometimes," she says, "there are Americans that don't want us to speak Spanish, or who say, 'Why don't you go back where you came from.' But really, they don't know what they're talking about. They talk because they have a mouth. They don't really know why we're here."

Relations between Mexican immigrants and native-born Americans at school has been positive, says Luisa. Though Luisa says she has American friends as well as Mexican immigrant friends, she points out that having been in English as a Second Language courses with the immigrant group since elementary school created a bond she has not been able to duplicate with her American-born classmates. Though friendly and outgoing, Luisa says it does not bother her if she cannot be friends with absolutely everybody.

LUISA: There are people who aren't going to like you. If they don't like me, it's not my problem. In school, I do have female friends, but I don't have girlfriends like I have guy friends. I get along better with men. Women are more problematic! A teeny little problem, and they like to make a big deal out of it. My friends are mostly Mexicans. Yes, I have American friends, but I get along better with the Mexicans. Because since we were seven, we have been together. We've been together in ESL, almost all Hispanics, we are always together more.

When she started high school, her mother began to move Luisa and her sister between trailer and apartment, and then back again. Switching high school districts each time, Luisa found it impossible to keep her studies in order. Some family friends, an American husband with a Mexican wife, invited her to move in with them.

LUISA: They treat me really well, as though I were their daughter. They worry a lot about me. They are like parents. They have helped me a lot, economically, emotionally—when I've most needed emotional support for the problems I've had, they have been there. They listen to me, they advise me, they scold me. Sometimes Mike drops me off at work, and every day he brings me to school. He really loves my sister and me a lot. He worries a lot about us. He wants the best for us, but at the same time he lets us be ourselves. He respects my decisions, even if sometimes he doesn't like them. His saying is, "Good decisions, good results. Bad decisions, bad results." That's his phrase. He asks me how school is going, and tells me to keep working hard. He's always telling me to spend time with my friends, and he tells me not to get married too young. He always tells me to wait until I'm thirty.

Luisa says she is not sure whether she agrees with that last piece of advice. Either way, she continues living with Mike and María so that life can be as stable as possible for her to focus on school.

LUISA: I had problems in a math class and I failed. I don't know what happened, I think it was because of the frustration I had, but in school I never showed that I had problems. I was always happy, attentive, active, smiling. But inside, I did have some problems. It's the only class I've ever failed in my life.

After graduating high school, Luisa hopes to go to a nearby technical college to study computers. The question, of course, is whether she will be able to. "I still haven't gotten my papers," she explains. "They have made a lot of proposals about students who want to study in the university, but they still haven't arranged it. It would be great."

In the hopes of making a good impression, she has volunteered for several summers as a teaching assistant in summer school courses at the local college. She hopes that, once getting to know her, the school will be more likely to let her come study.

Luisa has not told any of her friends at school that she is undocumented.

LUISA: I can't know if they might have some ill will. As the saying goes, *caras vemos, caras no sabemos*—we can see the face, but we cannot know it. Sometimes I say to myself, "This person would never be able to hurt me, because he or she is honest." But you really never know. Some of my teachers do know I'm illegal, and they don't really care. I trust them enough to tell them. My American neighbors do know that I don't have papers, and they don't care either. Sometimes I ask them if they care, and they say, "No, you're our friend."

Even though she has no legal documents, Luisa is settled in the United States. It is in this small Georgia town that she has grown up, and she believes it is there that she will stay.

LUISA: I started to see that there was better education and a better future here for my kids, one day when I get married. And I also want to be able to continue studying. In Mexico, there are a lot of people who never make it to high school, or even to junior high, because of the economy there. I saw all of this, and here I get more opportunities and I have a better future. Of course, I do want to go to Mexico to visit my family. But not to live. Maybe I'll change my mind, I'm not sure. But right now, I don't want to go back.

If Luisa's undocumented status keeps her out of college, it will have been a first for the young woman—the first time her lack of documents will have caused a serious rift between her opportunities and those of her American-born friends.

> LUISA: Thank goodness I haven't had problems. I've played volleyball; I don't have papers and that doesn't stop me. There are a lot of things you can have even without papers, but you need papers for other things. Like to buy a house, you would have to find someone who will sign for you. Things like that. But really, I don't feel different.

Victor, the Future Algebra Teacher

Thank goodness for the law, says an undocumented high school student named Victor. The new law, that is. Victor spent all of high school thinking his goal of becoming a math teacher was out of reach due to his legal status. By his senior year, he was courted by three scholarship providers, none of which would actually let him apply unless he proved his residency. Universities would not let him enter. But, in this August 2001 interview, Victor was pleased to report that "The Governor just signed a law a month and a half ago that even people without legal status can go to university, paying the same price as residents here in Texas. So that was a big help for me, because before this, really, I thought I wasn't going to college at all."

Paying for college will be a binational affair. Victor's family members on both sides of the border are chipping in for his education. At the time of this interview, an uncle had already paid Victor's first semester tuition at Laredo Community College, and an aunt was about to deposit money in his bank account for books.

Just about everything in Victor's life, in fact, is binational. Though he has no legal documents, he crosses the border at least once a week. He speaks both Spanish and English without an accent, but he usually switches back and forth between them in any given sentence. He wants to be a math teacher in Texas, but his other favorite subject is Mexican history.

Victor was born in Nuevo Laredo, on the Mexican side of the border. When he was seven, his parents took him and his two siblings to San Antonio. "Our dad wanted us to have a better life, I guess," says Victor. "Like any father." In San Antonio, his father worked as a mechanic, but died young due to liver complications. It was then that his mother took her children back to the border, to Laredo.

VICTOR: When my mom was growing up, she had a local visa to cross each day and work near the border. Since she was twelve years old, she had been cleaning the house of the same woman. That woman practically raised her. When my father passed away, my mother went back to work for that same lady.

Though Victor's perfect English allows him to easily pass for a U.S. citizen, things are much more difficult for his mother. In 1999, he says, the Border Patrol began stopping buses on the road between the largely-Mexican area where he lives and the center of Laredo. His mother was asked to get off the bus and show her legal papers. When she had none to show, she was placed in a detention center.

VICTOR: She was in the detention center for two days until she called to say they had her. She was crying. We were all worried because she just didn't show up. My sister told me she was worried because mom simply hadn't come home. We had no idea where she was. We were waiting, waiting, waiting for the telephone call until finally it came. The next day she saw the judge, and then she was sent back to Mexico. That was August 2, and she didn't come back until December 5.

Victor crossed the border that year to spend his birthday with his mother but had to rush back to Laredo the next day. He had a commitment—"It was the ten-year anniversary of the community center, and were going to have some *danzantes*, some Aztec dancers, and some poetry reading. I had to be there because I was part of it."

It seems seldom, in fact, that Victor isn't "part of it." At his high school, he was on the student council, played in a musical group, and did *danzante*, Aztec dancing. He is a community center volunteer and travels to Nuevo Laredo at least once a week to help build a church there. He says that crossing back and forth without papers does not scare him. Speaking sophisticated English without an accent and carrying the air of a serious math student, he just tells the Border Patrol he is a U.S. citizen.

VICTOR: I guess I've never had problems with the border patrol. I go to Nuevo Laredo a lot, and I'm not afraid of them. Someone told me, "If you're scared, just remember that you don't have to say anything to them if you don't want to." I am not afraid. I guess I just trust in God that things will turn out all right. I have the confidence that I'm going to go and come back. Sometimes they don't even ask questions, they just say, "Go." Sometimes they ask, "Are you a citizen?" And I say yes. I have my school ID, but I've never actually had to use it.

His mother cannot cross freely back and forth as he can. "She is going to have problems in the future until she gets her papers," he says. "And there's no way we can get her papers until either I get married or she gets married. Which is something," he says with a hidden smile, "that we're not planning to do until later. Because hopefully, I'm going to keep studying until I get my degree."

Though he plans to get his degree from Laredo Community College, Victor's path to becoming a math major began on the other side of the border.

VICTOR: I was in Nuevo Laredo for kindergarten and first grade. Over there you have to learn the times tables, and it was pretty easy for me to learn them. In San Antonio, I guess I was the number one kid in my math class, because I already knew the times tables while the rest of my classmates were doing addition and subtraction. When I first came here, to Laredo, I was still ahead. But in high school, I met my match in math! I had my B's and I had my A's, but I still love math. I hate biology. Biology and I don't mix. History, I love history, especially Mexican history. I love reading the Bible, Mexican literature, Christian books, Aztec books.

Victor has given to Texas—he has traveled to Austin for student council conventions, organized community picnics in Laredo, and volunteered at City Hall. And now, Texas is giving to him—giving him the possibility of a college education so that one day, he might give Texas even more as a teacher.

Victor has given to Mexico, too, when he crosses the border each week to build churches in Nuevo Laredo. When he graduates college and becomes an Algebra teacher, it seems most likely that he will be teaching in South Texas, instructing Mexican-Americans and Mexican immigrants, all of whom, in turn, will contribute both to Mexico and to the United States. He does not know how or when he will gain the legal residency that will make being a teacher possible, but he is confident that, one way or another, he will achieve his goal.

In the meantime, he will continue to cross back and forth across the border. He is Mexican enough to make it across in one direction and American enough to make it across in the other. Each time he crosses to Mexico, he takes a risk—he risks not being able to come back to Texas, to the life he has led since the age of six. But Victor always insists he is not afraid. "I think the Border Patrol is made up of normal people like you and me," he says. "Crossing the border? No, that doesn't scare me at all. I guess I see myself as an American too—a new American."

1 George Vernez and Lee Mizell. "Goal: To Double the Rate of Hispanics Earning a Bachelor's Degree." RAND.

2 Ibid.

Chapter 5

Open Borders?

Has the Time Come to Establish a North American Community?

The short answer is "No!" But let's analyze U.S. America today.

Just before President George W. Bush's controversial speech in January, 2004, proposing changes to "make our immigration laws more rational and more humane," U.S. pollsters were already at work sampling current public opinion on the issue. One national organization, the non-partisan Pew Research Center, gave the people it polled the following three options:

> Immigrants strengthen our country because of their hard work and talents.

> Immigrants today are a burden on our country because they take our jobs, housing and health care.

> Don't know.

In this particular poll, forty-five percent responded positively (immigrants strengthen our country), forty-four percent negatively, and eleven percent expressed no opinion.[1] (When the same questions were used in a April 1997 poll, the results were: thirty-eight percent positive, fifty-two percent negative, ten percent no opinion.) Other similar polls reported varying results, depending on how their questions were phrased and what demographic segments were contacted.

Immediately following the presidential election in November, then Secretary of State Colin Powell and five other Cabinet members flew to Mexico City for high-level talks with President Vicente Fox and his senior aides. Giving legal status to millions of undocumented migrant workers in the U.S. certainly was one of the top issues discussed.

The prospects for smooth advancement of the "Bush doctrine" were not enhanced by the passage of "Proposition 200" in Arizona by a 56-44 percent margin in the 2004 election. The state initiative claimed to be aimed at keeping undocumented immigrants from voting and obtaining some government services.

These events underscore the intensity of the debate raging over various immigration issues. Bush acknowledged in his speech that the U.S. is "a nation that values immigration and depends on immigration," and that the present system has "millions of hardworking men and women condemned to fear and insecurity in a massive undocumented economy." He went on to say that this situation "is wrong. It is not the American way."

Across the nation, particularly in areas with large populations of Mexican immigrants, the arguments have grown heated. One group complains that "illegals" are uneducated, don't speak English, take away jobs from U.S. citizens, increase social welfare costs for education and healthcare, and elevate expenses of prosecuting immigrant offenders for "criminal" activities. "They don't pay their way," say the critics, "and besides, they all violated U.S. laws to come here uninvited."

Those on the other side of the issue point out that immigrant workers, including the undocumented, pay billions of dollars in sales and income taxes, and to "false" social security accounts (because payroll forms may require a social security number). "They do not get benefits from these social security contributions," they say, "so this money goes to the government." They also mention that Mexican migrants, many devout Christians, bring rich cultural values and a strong morality. In addition, they make invaluable contributions to the U.S. economy by doing hard, dirty, dangerous jobs, as well as the drudgery American workers don't want to do—mostly at very low wages, with few protections and benefits.

Our Immigration Policy is Broken

It's time for significant and meaningful reform. To those who still say "Not now," many like myself say "We must give credit to whom credit is due! And now!"

Immigrants take care of our children, our elderly, our sick. They grow and harvest our crops, and staff the meat packing and poultry processing industries. They build our roads, our schools, our hospitals. It's time to reform immigration laws and give dignity to millions of hardworking "New Americans," recognizing that they are, in many respects, already good citizens of the U.S.

Opposition to immigration is not new. Throughout the history of this nation, some people have opposed the influx of immigrants from around the world who came here to find a better life. They protested against the Italians, Germans, Greeks, and Irish. They were so concerned about the number of Chinese "coolies" that they forced legislation to keep them out. Opponents were up in arms over the Scandinavians, Japanese, Koreans, and Vietnamese. They worried about the number of "foreigners" coming from Central and South America.

Yet, the United States ultimately made a place for these immigrants, and was enriched by their cultural contributions, talents, and hard work. As columnist Bruce Walker notes, "We sometimes forget—it is easy to do—that the Italians, Poles, Jews, Greeks, and Irish who crossed the Atlantic were the best: the risk-takers, the hardy, the optimistic, the faithful, and the hard-working. Much the same can be said for Mexicans who enter the United States today."[2]

And no, there are not more Mexicans now than any previous immigrant group. The approximately 1.1 to 1.3 million undocumented workers who cross the border each year, contrasted to a total U.S. population of almost 300 million[3], amounts to about a third of one percent! The number of all undocumented Mexicans in the country—estimated at between eight and twelve million—is only about three to four percent of the national population.

Whether motivated by fear, prejudice, or honest concerns, the debate over whether or not undocumented Mexican workers should be allowed in this country is a moot point. *The reality is that they are here!* And it is not at all likely that they will be leaving, either by choice or force. As I pointed out in chapter three, rounding up and deporting some eight million undocumented Mexican migrants, millions of whom own property in this country, and millions of whose children are U.S. citizens—is not a realistic possibility. Attempting such a task would be like putting the proverbial genie back in the bottle.

For those concerned about border security issues, President Bush must redefine for U.S. Americans the term "security," and clarify that it does not come through isolation. For example, greater security will not come from sealing the borders to immigrants (including the undocumented) who contribute so much to our success. I agree with the astute observation of the 19th century Frenchman, Alexis de Tocqueville, that the USA is a "unique" nation of immigrants who agree on a few basic values.

U.S. leaders must remind our citizens of the meaning of words like "freedom," "equality," and "independence." If U.S. Americans are to have a future of even greater achievement—and I think we will—we must make a greater commitment to our time-honored values. Even while protecting ourselves from possible future terrorist attacks, we must be careful not to lash out irrationally against friends and partners and destroy our very foundation.

What, then, should the U.S. do? Both Democrats and Republicans have presented legislative bills that would legalize the undocumented, create an intelligent work program, and open a citizenship track. Implementing the "Bush doctrine" or the McCain-Kennedy proposal would be a good first step. Bush proposed a temporary guest-worker program for Mexican immigrants, including the undocumented already in the country. The plan would allow them to remain if they have jobs and to apply as guest workers. The renewable three-year work permits would also enable these guest workers (only those with no criminal offenses, of course) to start on the path to qualify for permanent legal status.

The McCain Kennedy proposal goes a step further and seeks to bring the immigration laws closer to reality by increasing the yearly legal immigration to 400,000 people. The proposal also would provide legal residence for immigrants already in the country, and a path to eventually applying for citizenship.

Why Does Mexico Have Such Great Needs?

The current flow of eager and willing Mexican workers into the United States in many cases is prompted by desperation. The extreme poverty and lack of opportunity in most of Mexico is one of the major causes of the migration. As President Bush noted during an appearance on the Bill O'Reilly television program on September 28, 2004, "If you make fifty cents in the interior of Mexico, and five bucks in the interior of the U.S., you're coming for the five bucks." He went on the say, "And so long as the wage differential is as big as it is, and so long as moms and dads feel the necessity to feed their children, they're going to come and try to make a living."

Why is the situation so desperate in Mexico? The people and natural resources of this once-rich region have been plundered from the time of Cortez. Colonial powers seized vast quantities of gold, silver, and other mineral wealth, using military force to impose the rule of kings, emperors, and nationalist demands.

Even after Mexico gained its independence, its history was still turbulent, with constant skirmishes between competing interests of successive dictators and presidents who gave lip service to democracy but ruled with an iron hand. For centuries, the story of Mexico was an unending tale of terror and despotism, conflicts and chaos.

The losers in every battle were the people. Just before and after the turn of the twentieth century when dictator Porfirio Diaz held Mexico in an iron grip for thirty-five years, the country's major industries were controlled by foreign interests, the illiteracy rate was at eighty percent, 439 of every one thousand infants born did not survive, and the average life expectancy was thirty years. More than fifty percent of all houses in the country were unfit for human habitation, and in the capital, Mexico City, sixteen percent of the people were homeless.[4]

In 1928, President Plutarco Elías Calles created the National Revolutionary Party, which became the Revolutionary Institutional Party (PRI), the world's most durable political entity. Its candidates became presidents for seventy-one years. During its one-party rule, the PRI, in the words of the *Wall Street Journal*, "managed little but the refinement of populist demagoguery."[5] In other words, the PRI promised big and delivered little. The publication also noted that currently "the real drain on growth is from Mexico's 'monopoly problem'...the grip of public and private monopolies on the economic infrastructure...staunchly defended by the old-line PRI party in congress."

During the PRI's years of presidential control, Mexico saw startling increases in corruption, influence peddling, violent crime (such as a wave of kidnapping in Mexico City), and politicians on the payroll of powerful drug dealers. During the 1988-94 administration of Carlos Salinas de Gortari, his highly-touted economic "miracle" turned out to consist more in the creation of twenty-one new billionaires than raising the Mexican people's general standard of living.[6]

A Major Step in a New Direction

Then came the election of Vicente Fox, which amounted to a major step in a new direction for Mexico. His amazing charisma and willingness to break all the paradigms gave the people a new glimmer of hope and a glimpse of vision for how change can come.

I'll never forget the sense of excitement that pervaded the atmosphere in the very first cabinet meeting of the new administration. Fox told a story about an ancient temple that kept a black cat chained to a pillar outside for centuries. No one knew why—it had become tradition. One day a scholar going through old records discovered that a high priest preparing for an important ceremony had ordered that a cat running underfoot in the temple be removed and kept out. He meant his "order" to be for one day, but his underlings kept obeying it as divine law for centuries!

Then Vicente Fox said, "We have all kinds of rules and regulations in this country that are not based on our constitution and have no basis in law. I want you all to go looking for these 'black cats' and you have my authority to 'kill' every one of them you can find!"

For the first hundred days every day was exciting and full of hope—maybe even the first six months, and to a lesser extent the first year. Then the opposition of the PRI, the leftist PRD, and other political forces resumed with a vengeance. Fox upset many, attacking corruption and denouncing those who condoned it; he championed the cause of the people—whom he called heroes—as few, if any, Mexican leader had done for decades. His announced goals were to raise per capita income to $7,000 versus the $4,000 that existed when he took office and to reduce extreme poverty by thirty percent.

In an interview with *Time* magazine in January 2004, he said, "I'm determined to leave behind a totally competitive Mexican economy for once that generates a much better standard of living and gives people stronger rights."[7] He also confirmed that President George W. Bush's proposal on immigration rights had sprung from discussions between the two when they were still governors of their respective states. Both leaders had high hopes to achieve meaningful immigration reform, and still do, I believe.

The terrorist attacks on the World Trade Center twin towers in New York on September 11, 2001, changed everything. In the months that followed, concerns for security and increased control of U.S. borders pre-empted all other issues. And it dashed hopes and proposed schedules for many other plans for economic development. As the U.S. military actions in Afghanistan and Iraq progressed, Fox observed that the U.S. had forgotten Mexico amid its concern over terrorism.

In the *Time* interview, Fox commented, "I understand that not just the U.S. but all democratic countries have to confront terrorism, and that has been America's priority the past two years. Now we also have to get back to bilateral relations. Too many important initiatives have fallen behind—like immigration reform."

While President Fox's overall popularity in Mexico may not be as high as when he was first elected, most of the people still believe he is honest and is sincere in trying to change the nation for the better.

As Thomas Friedman, writing in an op-ed column for the *New York Times*, observed: "Because it happened so peacefully, it's easy to forget that Mexico in one decade has gone through two remarkable revolutions. One of the oldest one-party governments in the world was eased out with ballots, not bullets, and a poor developing country lowered its tariff barriers and became America's second-largest trading partner."[8]

And *The Wall Street Journal* noted, "Mexico's economic outlook this year is the rosiest it has been since President Vicente Fox took office in July 2000…Bear Stearns Global Emerging Markets Watch reaffirmed its 2005 forecast of four percent growth and lowed its inflation forecast by one percentage point to 4.1%. The improvement is good news for both Mexico and the U.S… although the growth number is well below the country's potential of six percent or seven percent annually." And, the paper noted, the growth rate is also below what economists say a developing country needs to seriously chip away at poverty.

Nevertheless, said WSJ, "it is worth pointing out that during the Fox administration, Mexico's fiscal and monetary condition has improved dramatically." Writer Mary Anastasia O'Grady went on to say, "Mr. Fox has pioneered the new Mexican era of pluralism and his presidency is not likely to be remembered for much more than that. But setting the record straight is important."⁹

Cure the Cause, Not the Symptoms

Even if President Bush is successful in getting more immigration reforms, including an "amnesty" or legal recognition of undocumented Mexican workers presently inside the U.S., this will not amount to a long term solution for either country. The answer, many believe, is the emergence of the North American Community, a fully developed coalition of Canada, the United States, and Mexico. Not one nation. Not open borders but a coalition — a block of three independent countries working together.

In the new era of international economic competition, the neighbor nations of North America must work together to effectively compete with emerging behemoths like China, India, and the European Union. In response to Bush's proposed temporary guest-worker program for undocumented migrants living and working in the U.S., Fox has boldly envisioned a North American "bloc" of countries that could be the leading and most competitive group of nations in the world "by working together and, through that, be able to keep increasing the quality and the level of life of our citizens."

Earlier, Fox had created a flurry of startled attention by announcing that ultimately he favors open borders across North America, and he proposes the removal of all immigration barriers between Mexico, the United States, and Canada so that "in five or ten years, the border is totally open to the free movement of workers."

Arturo González Cruz, the Mexican Foreign Ministry's institutional liaison for northern border affairs, said access changes along the 1,940 mile U.S.-Mexico border were "necessary" to facilitate increased travel and trade. "I would like to see a border similar to the one that Europe has right now...where they have very common objectives. They have a common economy. We need to promote better coordination and cooperation between our countries." Travel across national borders in the European Union is unregulated, and citizens of EU member nations traverse borders as freely and easily as Americans cross state lines.

Although the comments by both Mexican leaders prompted cries of concern in the U.S., a number of think-tank scholars and international experts have given serious consideration to the formation of the North American Community. One major study, headed by Robert A. Pastor of the Center for North American Studies at American University, was called "Closing the Development Gap: A Proposal for a North American Investment Fund."

Pastor notes that Europe has considerable experience in seeking ways to reduce disparities in income between rich and poor countries. "During the last forty years," he says, "Europe experimented with many approaches to this problem, and it has had considerable success." Recognizing that "wide disparities are intolerable in a community," the member nations set out to strengthen the economies and raise the levels of development of poorer countries. As a result, Ireland, Spain, Portugal, and Greece all received large infusions of capital—to the tune of hundreds of billions of Euros—contributed from the other member nations.

Was it a success? Ireland achieved the highest growth rates of any member state. Its per capital GDP rose from only sixty-one percent of the EU average in 1986 to 96.5 percent a decade later, eventually soaring to 105.1 percent. The other three poor countries—Spain, Portugal, and Greece—also made significant progress. For example, Spain's per capita GDP rose from seventy percent of the EC average in 1986 to nearly eighty percent in 1999.

In each case, the poor countries made significant contributions to match part of the investment in their development, most of which was focused on infrastructure and education. And also in each case, a "sunset provision" was established for every funding program to provide help but not build dependency.[10]

How does this relate to a North American Community? Both Pastor and columnist Tom Friedman assert that a more stable, middle class, and democratic Mexico is in the United State's (and Canada's) best interests. It would expand markets for American goods, reduce the flow of illegal immigration, and foster stability on our southern border.

But such a block would require significant investment by the two stronger nations through a North American Investment Fund. Pastor envisions a scenario in which $170 billion would be invested in Mexico over the next ten years, assuming that Mexico undertakes the necessary reforms to develop a more effective education system, improve the collection of taxes, strengthen the rule of law, and continue economic reforms.

The investment fund would require contributions from the U.S. of $9 billion annually, another $1 billion from Canada, and Mexico would supply the remaining $7 billion. The goal of all this investment would be to shrink the wealth gap between Mexico and the U.S.

Mexico has come a long way, especially since the establishment of the North American Free Trade Agreement (NAFTA) on January 1, 1994. Political and economic reforms have produced real results. However, NAFTA was never envisioned to be more than a treaty allowing goods, services, and capital to move more freely.

"What NAFTA accomplished was to get Mexicans to think forward and outward instead of inward and backward," said Luis Rubio, president of Mexico's Center of Research for Development. "[But] NAFTA was seen as an end more than a beginning. It was seen as the conclusion of a process of political and economic reforms and was meant to consolidate them...not only did Mexico not have a strategy for going forward, neither did America."

Pastor has proposed a way out—deeper integration. Canada, Mexico, and the United States should go beyond NAFTA, he says, and start building a North American Community, which addresses continental issues, from transportation to terrorism, in a wider framework. It is time to start thinking out of the box—or maybe into a bigger box. "This situation doesn't have to end in crisis," declares Pastor, "but it will if Mexico, the U.S. and Canada fail to act."

Enlarging the Opportunity

The proposed North American Investment Fund, over a ten-year period, would invest in roads, telecommunications, and post-secondary education in Mexico. Amazingly, there is no highway today that runs directly from resource-rich southern Mexico to the U.S. border. Trucks must go through clogged Mexico City.

When the European Union brought in the poorer countries of Spain, Portugal, Greece, and Ireland, it didn't just say, "Okay, now you're in our free-trade zone, let the market rip!" Rather, the EU made substantial investments in roads and education in the four new states and narrowed their income gap with the rest of Europe, giving their workers incentive to stay home.

Imagine what would happen in Mexico if funds were invested in infrastructure development—building roads and bridges throughout the nation, connecting the poorer southern states with the rest of the country and to the U.S. border. Immediately there would be multiplied thousands of good-paying jobs to attract Mexico's underemployed work force. And with improved transportation, electricity and water supplies, foreign investment would be attracted away from the crowded border areas to tap the resources and labor of the interior.

But Mexico must not sit back and wait for U.S. America and Canada. In the meantime, there have been some encouraging things happening along the border. Recently there has been a resurgence of the border manufacturers known as *maquiladoras*, according to an Associated Press story in January, 2005. The manufacturing and assembly operations are again thriving, with companies planning $4.5 billion in investments for new or expanded operations in 2005.

According to Nancy Boultinghouse, marketing director for the McAllen Economic Development Corporation, the biggest reason for the comeback is distance—it costs much less to ship manufactured goods to the U.S. from Mexico than it does from China. "Shipping prices can outrun savings on labor," she says. Plus, Mexico has an edge on producing copyright-sensitive goods, since China's stance on trademark law is "murky."[11]

A cooperative 15 square-mile development called "Silicon Border" may soon begin construction in Mexicali to tap into the high-tech semiconductor industry, according to a *Washington Post* news story. Asia now makes about half the world's semiconductors and threatens to dominate the manufacturing and technology of these critical electronics components. This is a source of concern given the dependence of the U.S. economy on electronics. U.S. entrepreneurs say they'd like to keep part of the $214 billion annual world market in North America.

D. J. Hill, chairman of the Silicon Border project, says the infrastructure of the park will cost at least $400 million, and that a single semiconductor manufacturing plant can cost more than $1.5 billion. Mexico's President Fox is supportive of the project, and state and federal governments have committed more than $2 million to the design and marketing of the high-tech facility and are offering ten years' tax-free status to semi-conductor companies that move into it.[12]

"The Mexican government is seeking to ease tax burdens on those companies, as Asian governments do, because of the jobs and benefits they take to Mexico," said Eduardo Solis, Chief of Mexico's Office of Promotion and Investment. "We are very much committed to offering a competitive package so it works."

He also noted that U.S. experts who come to train Mexican engineers could "go home to California for dinner" which is a distinct advantage over plants in Taiwan. Since Mexico has long suffered a "brain drain" with many top engineers and scientists going to more lucrative opportunities in other nations, this project would offer those professionals a reason to stay in Mexico.

If it develops as planned, Silicon Border will demonstrate Mexico's ability to provide high-tech facilities and labor at competitive costs, with distinct transportation and shipping advantages. These higher paying positions, combined with the lower-skilled assembly jobs at the *maquiladoras* operations, could make it increasingly attractive for Mexican workers to stay home.

The most effective migration strategy is one that narrows the income gap. This is also good for business, wrote Tom Friedman, "because as Mexico grows, it buys eighty cents of every dollar of its imports from the U.S.—unlike China"[13] or other nations separated from us by oceans and long distance.

President Dwight Eisenhower once said, "If a problem can't be solved as it is, enlarge it." Right now Mexico does not have the resources or political consensus to reform itself, and the U.S. does not have a strategy for managing immigration or its relationships with its neighbors. Indeed, some segments of the U.S. political system are still debating whether or not NAFTA was a good idea! Neither nation will solve its problem without a larger canvas. The unfortunate truth is that the U.S.-Mexico relationship has been drifting aimlessly, and the problem won't get smaller until the thinking gets bigger.

It's time to "enlarge" our thinking. It is time to think in North American terms—Mexico, the U.S., and Canada. The undocumented in the U.S. are not the problem. Our small thinking is the problem. Let's go back to our roots and think big.

1   "Politics and Values in a 51-48% Nation," Trends 2005, The Pew Research Center, Washington, D.C., January 24, 2005.

2   Bruce Walker, "How President Bush will transform the world," enterstageright.com, October 16, 2000.

3   POPclocks, U.S. Census Bureau, Population Division.

4   Jim Tuck, The Mexican Revolution, "A Nation in Flux," online Mexconnect.com.

5   Mary Anastasia O'Grady, "Blame Mexico's PRI-Era Monopolies for Slow Growth," The Wall Street Journal Online, January 28, 2005, p. A9.

6   Jim Tuck, High Hopes, Baffling Uncertainty, "Mexico Nears the Millennium," online Mexconnect.com, 1999.

7   "10 Questions for Vicente Fox," TIME, January 19, 2004, p. 8.

8   Thomas L. Friedman, "Out of the Box," New York Times, April 4, 2004.

9   O'Grady, The Wall Street Journal, January 28, 2005.

10 Robert A. Pastor, "Closing the Development Gap: A Proposal for a North American Investment Fund," Center for North American Studies, American University, 2004.

11 Lynn Brezosky, "Mexican border in business: Proximity to U.S. gives factories edge over Asian rivals," The Associated Press, January 16, 2005.

12 Mary Jordan, "U.S. looks to plant tech firms in Mexico," The Washington Post, December 20, 2004.

13 Thomas Friedman, "Out of the Box," New York Times, April 4, 2004.

Appendix #1

About the Author

Born in Forth Worth, Texas, the son of a Mexican father and a North American mother, Juan Hernandez has always had one foot in the U.S., and the other in Mexico. He spent most of his childhood in Guanajuato, Mexico, attended the University of Guanajuato, Lawrence University in Wisconsin, and later earned an M.A. and Ph.D. in English and Mexican Letters from Texas Christian University in Fort Worth, Texas.

In 1996, Dr. Hernandez founded the Center for U.S.-Mexico Studies at the University of Texas at Dallas and invited the Governor of Guanajuato, Vicente Fox, as a guest speaker. During the visit, Hernandez coordinated the first meeting between governors Vicente Fox and George W. Bush. Unbeknownst to Dr. Hernandez, the event would have a dramatic impact on his personal future and the outlook of Mexico-U.S. relations for years to come.

Juan quickly became an important part of Fox's team. In 1997 Governor Fox invited him to help with the creation of the Guanajuato Trade Offices, a project designed to establish trade offices in the U.S. representing the Mexican state. When Fox decided to run for president of Mexico, Juan was by his side … and continued by his side, as scheduler, confidant and unofficial chief of staff, for over three years of campaigning.

After the historic victory of the 2000 presidential campaign, Hernandez was appointed the head of the President's office for Mexicans Living Abroad, a position created especially for Juan, which also made him the first Mexican cabinet member ever to be a U.S. American citizen. While in office, Dr. Hernandez fought to end border violence, led informational campaigns on the dangers of border crossings, and fought to garner much due respect and recognition for Mexicans living abroad. In addition, Dr. Hernandez helped establish programs of the U.S.-Mexico Partnership for Prosperity, which sought capital investment for infrastructure and educational improvements in Mexico's poorest regions.

Dr. Hernandez was named one of the "Smartest People We know" when he was featured on the cover of *Fortune Magazine*, honored as "Humanitarian of the Year" by *Latin Trade*, listed as one of the "100 most influential Hispanics" by *Hispanic Business* magazine and one of the "100 most powerful Latinos" by *Poder* Magazine. Still a man with one foot on each side of the border, Dr. Hernandez is a regular guest on Univisión, ABC and Fox News.

Appendix #2

Declaration of Migrants' Rights and States' Responsibilities[1]

Revised by the "International Working Group on Migration" during proceedings on July 12, 2002 at The University of Texas Panamerican
Edinburg, Texas

WHEREAS throughout human history, lack of opportunity and hostile conditions in some countries, and demand for labor in others, have caused people to move from one land to another,

WHEREAS sending and receiving countries have significant mutual interests related to migration, but lack developed capacity to jointly manage these issues for mutual benefit,

WHEREAS any such joint management must further the democratic value of free movement and acknowledge the increasing desire of migrants to participate in more than one country at once, while respecting the right and obligation of states to control their borders,

WHEREAS migration management is a crucial for the promotion of national security in receiving societies,

MIGRANT SENDING AND RECEIVING COUNTRIES will have the following rights and responsibilities[2]:

1) The demand for immigrant labor implies that receiving countries do have responsibility to ensure the rights of immigrants.[3]

Immigrant-sending countriesmust work to change the social and economic conditions that caused emigration, and must strive to create opportunities for their citizens at home.

Sending and receiving countries should establish working relations and the institutions needed to manage their mutual migration issues. This is not an imposition on sovereignty, but rather a responsible exercise of stewardship.

2) Receiving countries should regularize the status of undocumented migrants, in order to build a society where identity fraud does not thrive, where border control is both economically and socially feasible, and where immigrants participate actively in the host society, rather than hiding in its shadows.

3) Sending countries and receiving countries should work together to create reliable and mutually recognized systems for those who live abroad to establish their identities.

Sending countries must find ways to establish the identities and permit the return of conationals whose identity documents have been destroyed during migration.

4) Sending and receiving countries should work together to facilitate the efficient, secure, legal and inexpensive transfer of voluntary remittances and other forms of assistance, from migrants to their families and communities of origin.

Both governments should create policies ensuring transparency and productive competition in the remittance-sending industry.

The primary purpose of remittances is to benefit migrants and their families, and as such they must not be taxed nor put to use for other projects, no matter how valuable, without migrants' consent.

Nonetheless, both governments should provide opportunities and incentives for migrants to invest these remittances in their communities of origin.

5) Sending countries should not see the process of migrants' incorporation into receiving societies as an identity threat and should allow for dual or multiple belongings, nationalities or citizenships, and the ability to exercise their political rights, wherever they may reside.

Receiving countries should not consider these continued residual attachments as threats to the full incorporation of new immigrants into the host society, but rather, should acknowledge that by permitting these multiple attachments, they not only facilitate social incorporation, but also enrich their societies

6) Sending countries that have a significant percentage of their populations living outside their national borders should include the concerns of emigrants and diasporas in their framework for creating and evaluating public policies.

Sending and receiving countries share the responsibility for informing migrants of their rights.

Sending and receiving countries should create mechanisms of democratic participation and representation for their immigrant, emigrant and diaspora populations.

Sending and receiving countries should re-examine their citizenship policies, and should move them towards the ultimate goal of permitting dual citizenship.

7) The consular protection rights guaranteed in the Vienna Convention are only the beginning of sending countries' responsibility to protect their co-nationals abroad; They should be encouraged to send representatives to ensure that all the basic rights guaranteed by the international community[4] are enjoyed by their emigrants.

Receiving countries must recognize these sending-country representatives as having a legitimate interest in protecting not only the persons but also the basic rights and dignity of these co-nationals.

1 This document has been presented by Dr. Juan Hernández at the Metropolis Conference "Diaspora and Homeland" in Dubrovnik, Croatia, in May 2002l, and at the conference "Sending and Receiving Countries in a World of Migration" in Edinburg, Texas, in July, 2002. Gratitude is due to the following individuals who have offered commentaries and suggestions. Their institutions are provided for identification purposes only: Jorge Bustamante (Notre Dame University), Alejandro Carrillo-Castro (National Institute for Public Administration, Mexico), Alberto Dávila (University of Texas Panamerican), Omar de la Torre (Government of Mexico), Howard Duncan (Metropolis Project), Jorge Durand (University of Guadalajara), Luin Goldring (York University), Khalid Koser (University College London), Amanda Levinson (University of Texas), Demetrios Papademetriou (Migration Policy Institute, Washington, D.C.), José Angel Pescador (El Colegio de Sinaloa), Mario Riestra (Conofam, Mexico), Neil Ruiz (Massachussetts Institute of Technology), Patricia Santo Tomas (Government of the Philippines), Yossi Shain (Georgetown University), Robert Smith (Barnard College), Joanne Van Selm (Migration Policy Institute), Leslie Voltaire (Government of Haiti), Julie Weise (Yale University).

2 Countries of transit also must afford human rights and basic protections to those migrants who pass through their territory.

3 These rights are spelled out in international conventions including: The International Convention on the Protection of the Rights of All Migrant Workers and their Families (U.N.), Universal Declaration of Human Rights, International Covenant on Economic, Social and Cultural Rights, International Covenant on Civil and Political Rights, International Convention on the Elimination of All Forms of Discrimination Against Women, International Convention on the Elimination of All Forms of Racial Discrimination, International Convention Against Torture and Other Cruel, Inhuman or Degrading Treatment and Punishment, International Convention on the Rights of the Child, ILO Migration for Employment Convention, ILO Migrant Workers Convention, ILO Forced Labour Convention, ILO Freedom of Association and Protection of the Rights to Organize Convention, ILO Equal Remuneration Convention, ILO Discrimination Convention, ILO Minimum Age Convention, Vienna Convention on Consular Relations, among others.

4 Ibid.

Appendix #3

The White House, Washington, DC
March 22, 2002

U.S.-Mexico Partnership for Prosperity

President George W. Bush and President Vicente Fox today welcomed a concrete action plan to promote economic development in the parts of Mexico where growth has lagged and fueled migration. **Origins of the U.S.-Mexico Partnership for Prosperity** When they first met as Presidents, in February 2001, President Bush and President Fox explained that, 'Among our highest priorities is unfettering the economic potential of every citizen, so each may contribute fully to narrowing the economic gaps between and within our societies.' In September of 2001, during President Bush's first state visit, President Bush and President Fox took an important step toward realizing that vision. They launched the Partnership for Prosperity, a private-public alliance to harness the power of the private sector to foster an environment in which no Mexican feels compelled to leave his home for lack of jobs or opportunity. After six months of work, the Partnership has produced a concrete action plan. The plan draws upon the best ideas emerging from two conferences (one in Merida, Mexico and one in Washington, D.C.) attended by over one hundred experts from the private and public sectors. The Partnership has been led in the United States by Deputy Treasury Secretary Kenneth Dam and Under Secretary of State Alan Larson.

Leveraging the Resources and Expertise
of the Private Sector

The action plan builds on the President's New Compact for Development. As President Bush said last week before the Inter-American Development Bank, "Most of the money for development does not come from aid. It comes from domestic investment, foreign direct investment, and, especially, from trade." The action plan, therefore, seeks to leverage private sector resources and expertise.

Action Plan

The action plan includes projects to facilitate investment in small business, housing, agriculture, roads, ports, airports, and information technology. Specific examples include:

- Increasing investment in housing. The U.S. Treasury Department will coordinate the provision of technical assistance to Mexico's Sociedad Hipotecaria Federal (SHF) to encourage securitization of mortgages and the creation of a secondary mortgage market in Mexico. In these efforts, Treasury will draw upon experts with experience in housing finance from private financial institutions, government-sponsored agencies (like Fannie Mae, Freddie Mac, and Ginnie Mae), and the U.S. Office of Federal Housing Enterprise and Oversight (OFHEO).

- Investing in infrastructure for commerce. The Partnership will lead an effort to spur the participation of U.S. companies in the development of Mexican infrastructure projects including: ports, an air cargo facility, and an expansion of Mexico's internet connectivity.

- Financing U.S. franchise opportunities for Mexican entrepreneurs. A U.S. franchise can be more than a brand-name, it can also be a set of best practices. As U.S. businesses share more of their business practices, technology, and distribution systems with Mexican entrepreneurs, productivity in the Mexican economy will rise.

- Supporting small businesses in Mexico. The Partnership, through the Small Business Administration and other agencies, will provide assistance in establishing small business development centers in Mexico to promote entrepreneurial competitiveness.

- Lowering the cost of sending money home. Last year, Mexicans and Mexican-Americans in the U.S. sent $9.3 billion home to family and friends in Mexico. But they paid high fees to do so. More competition in financial services will lower the fees and help make sure that more money gets to the people who need it most and helps strengthen regional economies. Also, U.S. Treasurer Rosario Marin will work to highlight awareness of competitive products by promoting financial literacy and expanded use of the banking system by American Hispanics.

Next Steps

Just as President Bush called for more accountability in development, the action plan calls on the Partnership for Prosperity to hold itself accountable for producing results.

Accordingly, the Partnership will continue and oversee the implementation of the action plan. In six months, the Partnership will report its progress. Drawing on President Bush's Management Reform Agenda, the Partnership will rate itself using a traffic light system of red, yellow, and green lights:

- The principal measure of the Partnership's success will be productivity - whether the Partnership succeeds in unfettering the economic potential of people in the parts of Mexico where growth has lagged and fueled migration.

- The Partnership will also rate itself on the degree to which it is led by private sector participants, ideas, and projects.

- Finally, the Partnership will rate itself on the speed of the implementation.

Appendix #4

Joint Statement by President Bush, President Fox, and Prime Minister Martin

Mexico, U.S. and Canadian Leaders' Statement and companion Security Agenda and Prosperity Agenda _ announcing the establishment of the Security and Prosperity Partnership of North America (SPP) _ were released at the conclusion of the trilateral summit at Baylor University in Waco, Texas.

SECURITY AND PROSPERITY PARTNERSHIP OF NORTH AMERICA

We, the elected leaders of Canada, Mexico, and the United States, gather in Texas to announce the establishment of the Security and Prosperity Partnership of North America.

Over the past decade, our three nations have taken important steps to expand economic opportunity for our people and to create the most vibrant and dynamic trade relationship in the world. Since September 11, 2001, we have also taken significant new steps to address the threat of terrorism and to enhance the security of our people.

But more needs to be done. In a rapidly changing world, we must develop new avenues of cooperation that will make our open societies safer and more secure, our businesses more competitive, and our economies more resilient3

Our Partnership will accomplish these objectives through a trilateral effort to increase the security, prosperity, and quality of life of our citizens. This work will be based on the principle that our security and prosperity are mutually dependent and complementary, and will reflect our shared belief in freedom, economic opportunity, and strong democratic values and institutions. Also, it will help consolidate our action into a North American framework to confront security and economic challenges, and promote the full potential of our people, addressing disparities and increasing opportunities for all.

Our Partnership is committed to reach the highest results to advance the security and well-being of our people. The Partnership is trilateral in concept; while allowing any two countries to move forward on an issue, it will create a path for the third to join later.

Advancing our Common Security

We will establish a common approach to security to protect North America from external threats, prevent and respond to threats within North America, and further streamline the secure and efficient movement of legitimate, low-risk traffic across our shared borders. As part of our efforts, we will:

- Implement common border security and bioprotection strategies;

- Enhance critical infrastructure protection, and implement a common approach to emergency response;

- Implement improvements in aviation and maritime security, combat transnational threats, and enhance intelligence partnerships; and

- Implement a border facilitation strategy to build capacity and improve the legitimate flow of people and cargo at our shared borders.

Advancing our Common Prosperity

We will work to enhance North American competitiveness and improve the quality of life of our people. Among other things, we will:

- Improve productivity through regulatory cooperation to generate growth, while maintaining high standards for health and safety;

- Promote sectoral collaboration in energy, transportation, financial services, technology, and other areas to facilitate business; and invest in our people;

- Reduce the costs of trade through the efficient movement of goods and people; and

- Enhance the stewardship of our environment, create a safer and more reliable food supply while facilitating agricultural trade, and protect our people from disease.

Next Steps

We will establish Ministerial-led working groups that will consult with stakeholders in our respective countries. These working groups will respond to the priorities of our people and our businesses, and will set specific, measurable, and achievable goals. They will identify concrete steps that our governments can take to meet these goals, and set implementation dates that will permit a rolling harvest of accomplishments.

Within 90 days, Ministers will report back to us with their initial report. Following this, the groups will report on a semi-annual basis. Because the Partnership will be an ongoing process of cooperation, new items will be added to the work agenda by mutual agreement as circumstances warrant.

Through this Partnership, we will ensure that North America remains the most economically dynamic region of the world and a secure home for our people in this and future generations.

SECURITY AND PROSPERITY PARTNERSHIP OF NORTH AMERICA

SECURITY AGENDA

We are launching the next generation of our common security strategy to further secure North America and ensure the streamlined movement of legitimate travelers and cargo across our shared borders. To this end, Canada, the United States, and Mexico will work together to ensure the highest continent-wide security standards and streamlined risk-based border processes are achieved in the following priority areas:

Secure North America from External Threats

- Develop and implement a North American traveler security strategy, to include consistent outcomes with compatible processes, for screening prior to departure from a foreign port and at the first port of entry to North America.

- Develop and implement a North American cargo security strategy to ensure compatible screening methods for goods and cargo prior to departure from a foreign port and at the first point of entry to North America.

- Develop and implement a North American bioprotection strategy to assess, prevent, protect, detect, and respond to intentional, as well as applicable naturally occurring threats to public health and the food and agriculture system.

Prevent and Respond to Threats within North America

- Develop and implement a strategy to enhance North American maritime transportation and port security.

- Develop and implement a strategy to establish equivalent approaches to aviation security for North America.

- Develop and implement a comprehensive North American strategy for combating transnational threats to the United States, Canada, and Mexico, including terrorism, organized crime, illegal drugs, migrant and contraband smuggling and trafficking.

- Enhance partnerships on intelligence related to North American security.

- Develop and implement a common approach to critical infrastructure protection, and response to cross-border terrorist incidents and, as applicable, natural disasters.

Further Streamline the Secure Movement of Low-risk Traffic across our Shared Borders

- Develop and implement a border facilitation strategy to build capacity and improve the legitimate flow of people and cargo at ports of entry within North America.

- Identify, develop, and deploy new technologies to advance our shared security goals and promote the legitimate flow of people and goods across our borders.

SECURITY AND PROSPERITY PARTNERSHIP OF NORTH AMERICA PROSPERITY AGENDA

Promoting Growth, Competitiveness and Quality of Life

To enhance the competitive position of North American industries in the global marketplace and to provide greater economic opportunity for all of our societies, while maintaining high standards of health and safety for our people, the United States, Mexico, and Canada will work together, and in consultation with stakeholders, to:

Improve Productivity

• **Regulatory Cooperation to Generate Growth**

- Lower costs for North American businesses, producers, and consumers and maximize trade in goods and services across our borders by striving to ensure compatibility of regulations and standards and eliminating redundant testing and certification requirements.

- Strengthen regulatory cooperation, including at the onset of the regulatory process, to minimize barriers.

• **Sectoral Collaboration to Facilitate Business**

- Explore new approaches to enhance the competitiveness of North American industries by promoting greater cooperation in sectors such as autos, steel, and other sectors identified through consultations.

- Strengthen North America's energy markets by working to-gether, according to our respective legal frameworks, to in-crease reliable energy supplies for the region's needs and de-velopment, by facilitating investment in energy infrastructure, technology improvements, production and reliable delivery of energy; by enhancing cooperation to identify and utilize best practices, and to streamline and update regulations; and by pro-moting energy efficiency, conservation, and technologies such as clean coal, carbon capture and storage, hydrogen and renew-able energy.

- Improve the safety and efficiency of North America's transporta-tion system by expanding market access, facilitating multimodal corridors, reducing congestion, and alleviating bottlenecks at the border that inhibit growth and threaten our quality of life (e.g., expand air services agreements, increase airspace capacity, ini-tiate an Aviation Safety Agreement process, pursue smart border information technology initiatives, ensure compatibility of regu-lations and standards in areas such as statistics, motor carrier and rail safety, and working with responsible jurisdictions, develop mechanisms for enhanced road infrastructure planning, includ-ing an inventory of border transportation infrastructure in major corridors and public-private financing instruments for border projects).

- Work towards the freer flow of capital and the efficient provision of financial services throughout North America (e.g., facilitate cross-border electronic access to stock exchanges without com-promising investor protection, further collaboration on training programs for bank, insurance and securities regulators and super-visors, seek ways to improve convenience and cost of insurance coverage for carriers engaged in cross border commerce).

- Stimulate and accelerate cross-border technology trade by pre-venting unnecessary barriers from being erected (e.g., agree on mutual recognition of technical requirements for telecommunications equipment, tests and certification; adopt a framework of common principles for e-commerce).

- **Investing in our People**
  - Work through the Partnership for Prosperity and the Canada-Mexico Partnership to strengthen our cooperation in the development of human capital in North America, including by expanding partnerships in higher education, science, and technology.

Reduce the Costs of Trade

- **Efficient Movement of Goods**
  - Lower the transaction costs of trade in goods by liberalizing the requirements for obtaining duty-free treatment under NAFTA, including through the reduction of "rules of origin" costs on goods traded between our countries. Each country should have in place procedures to allow speedy implementation of rules of origin modifications.

  - Increase competitiveness by exploring additional supply chain options, such as by rationalizing minor differences in external tariffs, consistent with multilateral negotiation strategies.

- **Efficient Movement of People**
  - Identify measures to facilitate further the movement of business persons within North America and discuss ways to reduce taxes and other charges residents face when returning from other North American countries.

Enhance the Quality of Life

- **Joint Stewardship of our Environment**
  - Expand cooperative work to improve air quality, including reducing sulphur in fuels, mercury emissions, and marine emissions.

- Enhance water quality by working bilaterally, trilaterally and through existing regional bodies such as the International Boundary and Water Commission and the International Joint Commission.

- Combat the spread of invasive species in both coastal and fresh waters.

- Enhance partnerships and incentives to conserve habitat for migratory species, thereby protecting biodiversity.

- Develop complementary strategies for oceans stewardship by emphasizing an ecosystem approach, coordinating and integrating existing marine managed areas, and improving fisheries management.

• **Creating a Safer and More Reliable Food Supply while Facilitating Agricultural Trade**

- Pursue common approaches to enhanced food safety and accelerate the identification, management and recovery from foodborne and animal and plant disease hazards, which will also facilitate trade.

- Enhance laboratory coordination and information-sharing by conducting targeted bilateral and/or trilateral activities to establish a mechanism to exchange information on laboratory methods and to build confidence regarding each other's testing procedures and results.

- Increase cooperation in the development of regulatory policy related to the agricultural biotechnology sectors in Canada, Mexico and the United States, through the work of the North American Biotechnology Initiative (NABI).

• **Protect our People from Disease**

- Enhance public health cross-border coordination in infectious diseases surveillance, prevention and control (e.g., pandemic influenza).

- Improve the health of our indigenous people through targeted bilateral and/or trilateral activities, including in health promotion, health education, disease prevention, and research.

- Building upon cooperative efforts under the International Conference on Harmonization of Technical Requirements for Registration of Pharmaceuticals for Human Use, work towards the identification and adoption of best practices relating to the registration of medicinal products.

March 23, 2005
Waco, Texas

Appendix #5

My Christmas List
(To Credit Unions)
By Dr. Juan Hernandez
(as appeared in the Fort Worth *Star-Telegram* on Jan. 5, 2005)

Walk into a bank or credit unions these days and you are increasingly likely to find yourself greeted by posters in Spanish, or in some cases even wall murals depicting Hispanic culture. Such symbols are a pragmatic recognition by financial institutions of the growing economic empowerment of Latinos in the United States.

But even as deposits by America's Hispanics increase exponentially, financial education for them about prudent money-management is woefully lacking.

I believe that institutions that reach out to America's Latinos in offering basic financial education services will find that gesture rewarded with both customer loyalty and greater deposits.

The fact is, Hispanics are now not only America's largest minority group, they are also America's fastest growing minority group. Hispanics consumers in America currently spend nearly $500 billion dollars a year. That's not chump change.

It is important to understand the barriers that sometimes prevent Hispanics from taking full advantage of America's good financial institutions.

So as my Christmas present to America's financial institutions, I offer this primer, in the form of a list of suggested small operational changes that can help secure the trust and loyalty of Hispanic depositors.

Clearly, one of those barriers is language. It is difficult for those who struggle with English to have the self-assurance to open an account and discuss financial transactions when that conversation is more likely to lead to confusion than to certitude. Imagine yourself trying to open a bank account in Paris with only halting knowledge of French. So the first request to financial institutions on my Christmas list is to try to ensure there is at least one person trained to speak Spanish in any branch of your institution.

Another barrier is trust. Long faced by usury rates for wire transfers and a sad history of exploitation in financial affairs, many Hispanics are slow to hand over to the wages of their hard-earned labor to institutions that have an impersonal remoteness and un-reassuring environment. So the second request on my Christmas list is for financial institutions to design remittance and deposit programs that take into account the unique needs of their Hispanic clients...and advertise those programs in a welcoming way.

Another barrier is knowledge of basic finance. True, many Hispanics have risen to positions of great wealth and influence in American society...lawyers, CEO's, major league baseball players and even Presidential counselors. But many more also perform lower-paying jobs that are nonetheless essential to keeping the wheels turning in the machinery that moves America: They help raise our children. They cook the food we eat in restaurants. They lay the tile in our kitchens and shingle the roofs of our homes. They harvest the crops we buy in stores every week. And yet, many have never received even the most basic education in money management. So the third request on my Christmas list is for financial institutions to offer and promote classes aimed at teaching the average Hispanic worker about interest rates, savings accounts, the power of compounding interest, how to analyze safe and higher-risk investments and when to choose which, and all the myriad methods of creating personal wealth. Financial institutions have a vested self-interest in implementing such policies.

When I worked with President Fox's Office running the Office of Migrant Affairs, I issued a regular report on institutions that were leading the way in offering competitive rates for wire transfers to help hard-working Mexican Americans and Mexican migrants get money to their families. My goal was to let America's Hispanics know who their friends are.

Through my partnership with the Texas League of Credit Unions and the Credit Union National Association, I am now making available to financial institutions advice and guidance on how to improve their services to America's newest, fastest growing economic power block, Hispanics. Contact me through my website, and learn how together we can create a Christmas gift for America's Hispanics that gives for a lifetime: The knowledge that leads to financial security and independence.

An Inch Measured in Light Years
By Dr. Juan Hernandez
(as appeared in the Fort Worth *Star-Telegram* on Feb. 13, 2005)

The immigration policies of Mexico and the United States are separated by an enormous divide of nearly an inch. Indeed, an immigration breakthrough is so attainable that failure may be almost certain. Such ironies exist when simple problems with simple solutions are complicated by politics.

Our two neighboring capitalist economies combine perfectly in forming the foundation for all economic success: Supply and demand.

America wants and needs labor (and intellectual capital), and Mexico helps provide it.

So what then, is the obstacle preventing implantation of a supply and demand-based immigration system?

Politics, essentially.

Some conservative Republicans are proving slow to recognize that the values, dreams and aspirations of American and Mexican Hispanics make them allies, not adversaries in building America's future … willing good neighbors, not "invaders" to be distrusted or feared. Some liberal Democrats speak as if borders and national sovereignty have no meaning at all. Each political party is driven to appeal to the historical stereotypes already established in the minds of their constituents, rather than demonstrate true leadership by fighting to change outdated or incorrect perceptions. The problem is, politicians don't win elections by picking fights with their most loyal voting blocks. Such practices are equally true in Mexico, where elected officials gain political favor with their constituents by being seen standing up to "obstinate" American lawmakers.

However, in the end, I believe that the market forces of supply and demand will prevail and drive the formation of a work-based bi-national immigration agreement.

Meanwhile, there is much that can do to advance bi-national immigration reform, and to improve the quality of life for people on both ends of the supply and demand process.

Three years ago, I began developing a declaration of "The Rights and Responsibilities of Sending and Receiving Nations." Developed in tandem with some of the world's leading immigration experts and organizations, we presented a core set of principles upon which we believe any fair immigration reform policies must be based.

The demand for immigrant labor implies that receiving countries do have responsibility to ensure the rights of immigrants.

Immigrant-sending countries must work to change social and economic conditions that caused emigration, and must strive to create opportunities for their citizens at home.

Sending and receiving countries should establish working relations and the institutions needed to manage their mutual migrations issues. This is not an imposition on sovereignty, but rather a responsible exercise of stewardship.

Receiving countries should regularize the status of undocumented migrants, in order to build a society where identity fraud does not thrive, where border control is both economically and socially feasible, and where immigrants participate actively in the host society, rather than living in its shadows.

Sending and receiving countries should work together to facilitate the efficient, secure, legal and inexpensive transfer of voluntary remittances and other forms of assistance, from migrants to their families and communities of origin.

Sending countries that have a significant percentage of their populations living outside their national borders should include the concerns of emigrants and diasporas in their framework for creating and evaluating public policies.

Sending and receiving countries share the responsibility for informing migrants of their rights.

Sending and receiving countries should create mechanisms of democratic participation and representation for their immigrant, emigrant and diaspora populations. (The percentage of Iraqi's in America who recently participated in choosing Iraq's interim government was truly extraordinary. It is a clear testament to the passionate affection many migrants hold for the democratic process in their native countries.)

While universal acceptance of an "International Immigration Declaration" may take longer to achieve, the differences in immigration policy separating the United States and Mexico are a divide much easier to bridge.

The USA can begin by creating a new class of work visa to encourage the fluid migration of Mexican nationals to job opportunities here. Mexico can collaborate with the USA to ensure that only those legally eligible to immigrate are doing so.

Both "good faith" first steps would require considerable political velocity in their respective nations to become law, but the benefits of success merit the risks by the legislatures of both nations. All that's needed for success is for elected officials to find new words to sell to their constituencies an old concept: Fairness. Let's make sure America's next immigration policy is as good as the people it reflects. Let's prove the inch currently separating a good immigration agreement between two great nations and peoples isn't too great a distance to travel to obtain justice.

Keeping Our Eye on the Prize

By Dr. Juan Hernandez
(as appeared in the Fort Worth *Star-Telegram* on Mar. 13, 2005)

Recently, I was invited to appear on Fox News Channel's "Hannity & Colmes Show," presumably to defend Mexican President Vicente Fox's Administration against claims they funded Mexican library books containing songs with passages that glorify drug dealers.

During the time I worked for Vicente Fox, I came to know what I believe is his heart. I also feel confident I know the heart of the Mexican people. As an American of Mexican heritage, working in the Mexican cabinet, I felt one of my principal goals was to foster harmony and reach new understandings between our two great nations.

That is why I have grown troubled in recent months by what appears to be growing efforts by special interests to highlight and sharpen divisions between the governments and the peoples of the United States and Mexico.

The Mexican government's funding library books with songs glorifying drug dealers has become one such point of controversy.

I believe the producers of "Hannity & Colmes" expected me to be an apologist for such a misguided idea. They were wrong.

Now, I know we are only talking about a few lines in a couple of songs. Nevertheless, I have no intention of excusing misguided decisions that may result in children being taught that drug lords are anything other than murderous, greedy, immoral merchants of addiction and death. Period.

Before going on the program, I did some quick research to confirm whether the information was true that Mexican government funds were, in fact, being used to buy books for libraries with songs glorifying drug dealers. After sadly confirming that it was true, I immediately phoned contacts in President Fox's administration to make them aware of this outrage, and was told that I could expect "heads to roll." They should, and I'm confident they will.

Not infrequently these days, people from both countries with il-licit private agendas will seek official sanction —and taxpayer fund-ing!—for promoting agendas that conflict with the public welfare. Such programs –when forced to rely on success in the free market-place—nearly always meet failure when the public expresses moral disapproval with their pocketbooks. Yet, deceptive ideologues and activists regularly slip educational materials past the noses of over-worked or inattentive government workers…educational materi-als that defy the values of their audience. It seems such was the case here. However, such episodes are not unique to Mexico, which takes us back to my point.

The average good citizen of Mexico is just as offended by such textbooks as we are in the United States. Let us not indict the ordinary citizen of Mexico, nor their honorable and conscientious President for the actions of a criminal subculture trying to corrupt the hearts and minds of Mexico's schoolchildren.

As a U.S. citizen and parent, I would not tolerate my state or fed-eral tax dollars being used to promote the values of a criminal ele-ment. Nor do I for one second believe that the hard-working, law-abiding, church-going people of Mexico want their tax dollars pro-moting the drug lords who make victims of their own children. The Mexican people are wise enough not to make heroes of crimi-nals who couch their misdeeds in nonsensical populist economic rhetoric.

I have been honored by a unique vantage point in my career as a political advisor: I have not only had the opportunity to help de-velop improved relations between the political leaders of Mexico and the United States, but also to get to know well the hearts of the average Mexican and the average American, too. And I firmly believe that whether the media, government bureaucrats, special interest groups or even a criminal subculture seek to divide the people of Mexico and the United States…in the end, I believe the bond that will unite our nations will be the common good in the hearts of the people inhabiting both countries.

I believe it is natural that nations, like individuals, complement and advance one another through the unique strengths of their respective cultures.

I also believe that Mexico and the United States are too good and too great of nations to be kept apart by the private agendas of special interests. We cannot allow unimportant sideshows to cause historic opportunities to pass…opportunities, for example, to reach breakthroughs in immigration and economic policy.

I think it's time we sent a message to our respective elected officials, insisting that progress resumes soon on a fair and honorable immigration plan between Mexico and the United States, and that a new paradigm is launched in economic relations.

It's time to remember that which binds us is great, and that which divides is small indeed. Let's keep our eye on the ball, and not be distracted by sideshows.

The Guanajuato Project

By Juan Hernández

(as appeared in the Fort Worth *Star-Telegram* on March 28, 2005)

President Fox and President Bush met this week for discussions concerning migration, national security, and trade issues. Though some have said that statements made by both were a let down, sometimes what goes on behind doors is more important than what is presented in a press conference.

In fact, this was a meeting between two men who have known each other since they were both Governors of leading states in their respective countries. Indeed, they conferred on bi-national issues when they were both candidates in the same year for President of their respective countries.

While I was working as a professor at the University of Texas at Dallas I was honored to have a hand in launching the friendship of these two leaders. In addition, I was privileged to have had the opportunity to subsequently arrange the next two meetings between the soon-to-be presidents. And let me tell you, what I heard them say before going out to the public was always more daring and promising. As everyone now knows, a fast friendship developed between these two leaders…both strong in their political convictions, but equally concerned about their own constituents.

During their meeting in 1996, and then in 2000, Vicente Fox proposed to Bush the creation of a Common Market-type relationship to replace the free-trade area, and volunteered the idea of a compensation fund for the poorest country of NAFTA's Mexican, Canadian, and American partnership. After inviting Bush to his ranch in February 2001, Fox persuaded President Bush to endorse "The Guanajuato Proposal," or "Partnership for Prosperity," a key part of which said: "After consultation with our Canadian partners, we will strive to consolidate a North American economic community whose benefits reach the lesser-developed areas of the region and extend to the most vulnerable social groups in our countries."

Progress along these lines was slow even before September 11th. The circumstances of that dreadful day brought to a screeching halt much of the aspirations for implementation of this goal. The simple fact is, new priorities took center stage. Prosperity cannot flourish where security proves elusive.

However, I believe that it is time for the leaders of the three nations to breathe life back into "The Guanajuato Project." The time is now to refocus our energies in building the most powerful economic bloc in history ... but to also use those resources to help build the most economically just system in history.

Such planning does not necessarily require hand-outs or even "hand-ups." It requires nations to first take stock of the internal political changes that are prerequisite to international investment...and then create incentives that unshackle the power of free-enterprise to do what they do best: create, innovate, sell, serve, and grow.

With recognition of Robert Pastor's thoughts and words contained in his paper, "Closing the Development Gap," here are some lessons learned from Europe's creation of a European Union that can guide our thinking on what may also work in building our North American consortium:

1. **Declare Goals.** Set goals of solidarity and community...a sense that each nation's respective populace would cooperate in new ways to bring peace and prosperity to all.

2. **Convergence.** Regional trading plans can be an effective vehicle for lifting middle income countries, particularly when greater uniformity in national policies is created.

3. **Reduce Volatility.** Richer countries need to find ways to cushion the economic swings that poorer countries suffer. Macroeconomic policy coordination and financial arrangements

should be undertaken to protect the poorer countries from foreign exchange crises.

4. Emigration. As the disparities between rich and poor countries were reduced in Europe, migration was significantly reduced...no small lesson for those concerned with the Mexican-American immigration issues.

5. Magnitude of Commitment. The task of closing the gap between richer and poorer countries in a free trade area is a formidable one, but is attainable provided its members made a serious commitment and appropriate significant funds expressly for that purpose.

President Reagan used to keep a sign on his desk that, in paraphrase, said, "We can accomplish great things, if we don't care who gets the credit."

What applies between individuals applies as well between nations, as America discovered from its successful rebuilding of post-World War II Europe under "The Marshall Plan." The sacrifice then of a generation of selfless Americans built a stronger, more secure, more prosperous world.

No, I am not saying that we should "open the borders." Nevertheless, we should think of North America as a block of three individual countries with many common interests. We have before us an opportunity to create the greatest economic engine in the entire history of the world — right here in our backyard. And as Americans, we hold the key. Our partners are willing. The time is now to engage the process. I believe the leaders of Mexico and the US are talking about this "behind closed doors." Now it's time for us in the public forum, and in the legislatures of both nations, to have the same discussion. The time is now for the Guanajuato Project.

John Paul II

By Dr. Juan Hernandez
(as appeared on April 10, 2005 in the Fort Worth *Star-Telegram*)

The population of Rome doubled overnight as millions of people of all faiths gathered to pay their final respects to the Pope. Even world renowned politicians struggled for relevancy, overshadowed as they now are by the record-setting news coverage of this great man's passing.

What made this Pope so beloved and controversial? What about him stirred such affection and respect in the hearts of so many?

In a word: Principle.

Because we live in a time when fame itself seems regarded as a virtue, a time when what is "politically correct" seems more greatly valued than truth, a time when no tradition remains unchallenged by radicals with agendas...Pope John Paul II's principled, uncompromising leadership stood out. In an era of rampant cynicism, this was a man unapologetic and unshakable in his adherence to his beliefs. Together with his humanity, it was, in largest part, the strength of his unfaltering convictions that drew us to him.

It is very clear that this was a man who long understood his mission, and who embraced it with courage. Unconcerned with society's wants, he had the courage to speak to what he thought were its needs.

Pope John Paul II believed that there is good and evil in our world, and he was unambiguous about proposing to us the distinction. The Pope judged communism to be one such evil because it not only suppressed basic human rights and freedoms, but also because atheism was an official communist policy. Believing freedom is a basic human right endowed by our Creator, the Pope rightly resolved there could be no room for compromise with such an ideology.

This Pope made clear that he believed there were eternal verities, and was criticized for it by some. His critics included those who believe if the teachings of Scripture are inconvenient to modern lifestyles, then the teachings should change to suit the times. It is clear this Pope never lost sight of who he thought his Boss was. And it wasn't us. He believed his first service was to the Truth, and by living his convictions, he served us all well.

Thankfully, this Pope needed no polls before presenting his views. However, in an unsurprising confirmation of this column's premise, a recent AOL poll revealed that a plurality of 29% of voters attributed their affection for this Pope to his strongly-held views. His role in the collapse of communism ranked second in their esteem at 21%, with all other considerations registering much less significantly.

Although both courted and denounced by world leaders, Pope John Paul II was not a "political" man by ordinary definition. Rather, his expressions of public policy were extensions of his faith…invariably stemming from his belief in the dignity and sacred essence of all people. He supported democracy and human rights for this reason. He opposed abortion for the same reason. He opposed war and the death penalty for the same reason. He also upbraided Liberation Theologians of Central America for embracing Marxism for the same reason.

Aside from his fellow Poles, that appreciation and reverence may scarcely be felt more deeply than by Mexicans, who were the beneficiary of five visits by the Pope. His humanity, his fervent commitment to life, his compassion for the world's poor, his devotion to human rights…all resonated with, and made him beloved by, Mexicans and Hispanics everywhere.

It was for this consistency and commitment to principle that people around the world appreciated and revered People John Paul II. Such is the power of conviction. Such is the power of principle.

Message to Congress: The Time Is Now To Lead On Immigration Reform

By Dr. Juan Hernandez
(as appeared in the Fort Worth *Star-Telegram* on May 8, 2005)

When it comes to immigration, it seems the chaos on the border is exceeded only by the chaos in Washington.

That is especially curious since Members of Congress are usually famous for being able to read which way the political wind is blowing. In this case, however, it appears they would be well served to commit to reading the results of a recent, reputable bi-partisan national survey of voter attitudes on immigration.

What its findings show is not at all startling, and is indeed testimony to the common sense of US Americans.

With solutions to border, immigration, and guest worker issues so logical and obvious, it can only be the handiwork of feuding Washington special interest groups to have befuddled and complicated what is clear and simple.

Most noteworthy for Congress among the findings is that two-thirds of all voters say they would be more likely to vote for a candidate who favors the type of immigration approach identified in the survey!

Here are highlights from the findings of a bi-partisan poll on immigration taken in March by Republican pollster Lance Tarrance, and Democratic pollster Celinda Lake, commissioned by the National Immigration Forum.

The survey shows that fully 75% of likely voters favor a proposal with the following components:

- Registration of undocumented workers as temporary guest workers,

- Temporary work visas for seasonal and temporary workers,

- Provides newly registered workers with a multi-ear process for legal residency and eventual citizenship,

- Provides newly registered workers with no preferential treatment for citizenship,

- Provides penalties for workers or employees who violate these laws

- Puts a priority on reuniting close family members.

Seems logical and fair enough! Which is undoubtedly why it enjoys the support of 78% of Republicans, 77% of Independents, and 70% of Democrats, and 70% of Hispanics and 78% of whites, alike. Moreover, 69% of likely voters said they would be more likely to support a Congressional candidate who favored a comprehensive approach to reform, rather than the ad-hoc, piecemeal approaches currently working their way through Congress. Enforcement-only strategies miss the point, and the majority of people recognize them for what they are: emotional reactions that do not recognize nor solve the problem. Everyone recognizes that the system is broken and needs to be fixed. But let's not make the cure worse than the disease.

Most Americans, including myself, have legitimate concerns about the need to keep our borders secure from terrorists. This is no trivial concern in a post-September 11th world in which our intelligence services continue to uncover evidence of terrorist intentions.

Our message to Congress should be this: "Let's prioritize this issue! Let's bring together the political leadership of both nations, immigration leaders, Hispanic leaders, and other interested parties to start hammering out the framework of a reform proposal that is comprehensive, bipartisan, fair and worthy of the people of two great nations. Why not create a U.S.-Mexico Congressional Summit in Washington, D.C. that brings some sanity out of the chaos?"

I believe it is time now for Congress to put the issue of immigration on a front burner before the next election cycle causes the issue to become mired in election-year politics.

Fair, pragmatic, bipartisan, comprehensive-yet-fairly-simple solutions are possible. The time is now for Congress to wake-up and lead on immigration reform. Survey results clearly show the American people stand prepared to politically reward those do so.

Contact:

Juan Hernandez
PMB 312
4750 Bryant Irvin Rd. Ste. 808
Fort Worth, TX 76132-3611

24 Hour TV Network: www.juanhernandez.tv
Website: www.juanhernandez.org